ROUND AND ROUND IN CIRCLES

CH00762365

ROUND AND ROUND IN CIRCLES

Peter Marsh!

Under the burgee of the
West Anglesey Nautical Cruising Association

An imprint of
ANNE LOADER
PUBLICATIONS

To Mother

ISBN 1 901253 12 0

Published November 1999

Published by:
Léonie Press
an imprint of Anne Loader Publications
13 Vale Road, Hartford, Northwich,
Cheshire, CW8 1PL Gt Britain

Designed by: Anne Loader Publications

Printed by: Transport Print, Unit 4, Brook Street Mill,
Turnock Street, Macclesfield, SK11 7AP

Cover illustration by: Ian Walsh

A BIT ABOUT THE AUTHOR

Peter Marsh was conceived in Looe on Christmas Day 1943 and born nine months later in Macclesfield, Cheshire, the eldest son of a handsome, dashing anti-aircraft gunner and his pretty young wife, a forces entertainer.

Much of Peter's youth was spent attending school. Then, in defiance of his father, who had become an estate agent when the threat of Hitler had been safely removed, Peter ran away to London and the heady world of advertising. Estate agency didn't appeal, although his father's love of sailing had already lured Peter into this most pleasant of pastimes. So, this was to be his life. Advertising... and sailing.

For much of his mis-spent adulthood, Peter has wagged off work, attending other people's boats, taking as much time as possible away from the hurly-burly, crewing on deliveries and off-shore races, as well as many weekends spent racing his ageing dinghies and off-shore pleasure sailing with friends. Latterly, advertising took a very far back seat as the desire to own his own craft finally became a reality and prompted this tale, the first in a planned trilogy revolving around the antics of Peter and his fellow yotties. Happy and sad tales, yarns not only of the sea, but of life itself.

Peter's personal probe into his desire to live life to the full, to observe and comment, and share those feelings with other like-minded folk, can only stem from the day of his conception. What were you giving on Christmas Day, 1943? Or any other Christmas Day for that matter?

'Round and Round in Circles' is the beginning of Peter Marsh's gift to a world which has been going round and round in circles for quite a long time. And will continue to do so for some time to come...

Hopefully!

i

CONTENTS

INTRODUCTION

There comes a time in everybody's life when one realises that what's left of the alotted time needs change, something different. A change of scene, maybe, or an alternative way of life. Anything, but it must be something. In men, it's popularly called 'mid-life crisis', for women, menopause.

Any excuse, but change takes place, engineered or otherwise.

I have spent my life on a treadmill, much as most of us do and, despite several attempts to bring about change, I still find myself on it. My particular treadmill is writing, most of my life having been spent in the advertising industry, interspersed with several unsuccessful attempts to get away from it.

This year I made yet another attempt, the boldest yet. This is the story of that bid for freedom, escape from reality, call it what you will. I engineered my break, it was a conscious decision, I wasn't pushed. And I always intended to return to the treadmill, but this time to plan the ultimate break, the final bid for freedom, the last step to the top of the ladder we call life.

Whether I will be successful in taking that step only time itself will tell. If you've read this far, and you must have been enticed by something, dear reader, then in your own small way you have helped me up towards the top rung – and my thanks.

Whilst all the tales told within are largely true, I've had to change some of the names of people and places in order to protect the innocent, as they say, and prevent my letterbox being filled with writs. I do hate being on the receiving end of legal mail and for that reason alone I have been advised to take this step. The folk I have slagged off, however, will almost certainly recognise themselves and I sincerely hope that they take note.

I should also mention here that, as many of the tales revolve around yottin', I have been obliged to use yottin' terminology, 'Yottspeak'. I make no apology for this — as some readers may well be yotties themselves, they will become quickly bored if I stop to explain the Yottspeak. The rest of you, I'm afraid, will just have to put up with it or refer to the 'Glossary of Yottspeak' at the rear of this tome.

Read and enjoy!

Peter Marsh
September 1998

Chapter 1

BLAME IT ON THE DOORSTEP

In which I attend the Cartoon Festival in
Arles, Provence, crash the hire car and have
a run-in with the police.

I was sitting quietly on my own, perched on a high bar stool, sipping coffee, I hasten to add. It was only 10.30 in the morning, and I was musing over coincidences.

For instance, the place I'm in is called Latitudes, a conference centre just outside Arles in Provence. And that's exactly what the barmaid had, *l'attitude* – and a bad one at that. I couldn't find one redeeming feature about this poor example of womanhood, and I wasn't even going to try. I'd just decided to finish my coffee and seek more pleasant company when I felt a hand on my shoulder

"Hi, Pete. Good you could make it."

It was my good pal Chris, a delegate at *Forum Cartoon*, the conference being held here at Latitudes. Hardly a co-incidence that we should bump into each other, he'd told me about the *Forum* a couple of weeks earlier when we'd gone out for a pint or two of stout. We'd arranged to meet when we were in O'Shea's, an Irish bar in Manchester and I'd treated Chris to a Dublin Doorstep, an enormous sandwich with bread an inch thick and stuffed with black pudding, bacon and tomatoes.

"It's in Arles," he'd said, in between giant mouthfuls and flying crumbs. "In Provence."

Now for some while I'd been promising myself a trip to Provence and investigating the possibility of at least a semi-permanent life there. Here was the perfect excuse. I'd returned home and booked a cheap EasyJet flight that evening.

"Hi, Chris," I replied. " Wouldn't have missed it for the world."

I stayed on the bar stool with my back to the barmaid and we were joined by Nick and Nigel, the two guys Chris was here with. We chatted for five minutes and they left for a last rehearsal of their presentation, the project they'd been working on for over six years.

I took one more look at the barmaid and found another bar.

12.20pm came soon enough, the time for the boys to present 'Skid' to the world of cartoon buyers.

I blagged my way into the conference room, telling the girl on the door that I'd left my badge in the hotel, and found a seat. I was the first in. Ten or so more arrived and the Chairman kicked off.

Despite my close friendship with Chris, we're both writers, we don't talk 'work' very much and I had little idea of his project, other than knowing it was kind of 'Thomas the Tank Engine with cars'. His description, and a very accurate one. I enjoyed the showing very much and the other delegates were not exactly rude about it. Some were very complimentary, but afterwards Nick and Nigel were very depressed and started rowing: 'We should have done this, we should have done that.' The usual reaction, but I didn't feel the same way and Chris agreed. It was early days, the first day of the conference in fact. Three more to go, and anything could happen. At least they'd got it out of the way. Now they could concentrate on getting close to the people who mattered. We went for lunch.

Same story for me on the door: I'd left my badge at the hotel. It was a great lunch with wine — and all free.

We shared our table with some other friends from Manchester, there to make two presentations, and co-incidence struck again. One of the other lads, Ben, who I'd known well for some years, told me he'd moved a few months ago, to a village in Cheshire, Little Budworth. I used to live in Little Budworth twenty years ago and I said so — in the cottage opposite the Church, next door to the pub. Guess which house Ben had moved to. We swopped stories about the cottage, the village, the pub and the people. Ben promised to invite me to his fortieth birthday party. Couldn't wait. It'd be great to see the old place again.

We watched another presentation in the afternoon and then I took the boys back to their hotel in my hire car, a green Ford

Fiesta. Nigel wanted to chill out on his own so, after they'd freshened up, Chris, Nick and I went out for a meal.

The night before, when I arrived in Arles, I'd asked a waitress in a terrace restaurant how to get to the hotel Chris had told me he was staying in. She'd never heard of it, so I'd gone in search myself. I couldn't find it and it was late, so I'd tried several hotels to book into myself. Could I find one? No. All fully booked — 'complet'. I'd walked back to the car, resigned to having to stay out of town, and passed the same restaurant. The waitress had come out onto the terrace and asked if I'd had any luck. She was very attractive, spoke good English and offered to find me a hotel room, then telephoned one of the hotels I'd already tried and got me straight in. I'd promised to bring my friends to the restaurant the following night. Any excuse to chat her up!

So that's where the damage started, in the Restaurant Medieval. Several *pastis* and wines later, with the odd lamb chop thrown in, we tried to order a taxi to get Chris and Nick back to their hotel a mile or so out of town, mine being just around the corner. We waited and waited, but no taxi. Slight bonus, in as much as it gave me a chance to chat up the waitress, Karine. She even gave me her address.

Eventually, I said I'd get the hire car and run them back to their hotel myself. Silly boy.

I woke up next morning wondering why, at the age of very nearly 53, I still had all the sense of an 18 year old.

It was the doorstep's fault. If I hadn't bought Chris the Dublin Doorstep, perhaps I'd never have been in Arles. And Arles has sticky-out doorsteps in its narrow, medieval streets. Slaloming up possibly the narrowest and darkest street, on the way back to the Medieval, I inadvertently didn't see one and it knocked off the front right wheel. Slewing round the next corner, the hire car ground to a halt and I legged it. No way was I going to tell the police, Lo-Cost Rent-a-Car or Europe Assist. That could wait until tomorrow, the aforementioned tomorrow that found me wondering about my sense — or lack of it.

In the last twenty years I've only had two car crashes, both in

France and both in green cars. Walking back towards the restaurant I realised that I should have demanded another car, a different colour.

I found Chris and Nick, still waiting for a taxi, gave them the bad news and they started walking back to their hotel.

"Somewhere near Les Arènes, I think."

That was about as specific as I could be in reply to the kind Europe Assist lady on the other end of the telephone line.

"Les Arènes. Zere are a lot of ze narrow street near Les Arènes, m'sieur."

"I know. I left the car in one of them." This conversation was going nowhere. "Look, I'll tell you what. I'll go and find the car, then ring you back. OK?"

"Une bonne idée, m'sieur."

Could I find it? Could I hell. It had gone. I tried every single damn street and eventually found a Ford hub cap near a doorstep that looked as if I wasn't the first not to have noticed it. It must have been several hundred years old though and let's face it, it was still there. Unlike the Ford Fiesta.

"It's gone."

"I know, m'sieur. It is wizz ze police. It is neccesaire for you to attend ze Police Station and pay ze fine."

My worst fear is of the police, particularly foreign ones. I felt myself going cold and I started to tremble. My mouth went very, very dry and my tongue stuck to the roof of it.

"Pardon, m'sieur, I do not unnerstan."

"Golice. Ghere? Golice?"

"At ze Police Station in Arles. You know where is ze Police Station in Arles?"

I've been asked some damn fool questions in my time, but this one took the biscuit. Suddenly I felt saliva. Must have been some sort of reaction.

"Course I don't f..., sorry, know. I haven't been here more than a day. You're lucky I knew where Les Arènes was and I'm a lot more interested in sightseeing than passing time with le fuzz."

"Le what?"

4

"Fuzz, dear girl. *Les flics*, the boys in blue."

"*M'sieur*, you go to Boulevard Des Lices. Ze Police Station, it is zere. You pay ze fine and ze towing charge and I will try to get you anuzzer car now."

She was a tad icy, but then she wasn't to know who she was dealing with, a complete dithering coward, nearly 53 and no sense.

The aptly named Boulevard Des Lices did indeed have a Police Station, and a *Gendarmerie* which I imagined had dank cells. It was warm outside in the Provençal sun. I stood for a while, smoking what I thought would be my last cigarette for some time, perhaps my last ever. Eventually I made my way up the disabled people's ramp which wound its way alongside the steps. It took probably seconds longer, but now every second was one of freedom. At the top I stopped and put my hand on the doorknob. I was just about to take a deep breath when a reflection in the glass door caught my eye. It was a blue uniform, a very shapely blue uniform, not what you'd expect really. In a holster, hanging from the belt which hugged a very narrow waist, was a pistol, languishing on a perfectly rounded hip. The hips swayed closer and the voice behind me was silky, husky.

"*M'sieur*, You are wanting ze Police? You are English, yes?"

My eyes couldn't leave the gun, or rather the reflection of the gun. I was transfixed.

"Yes. Yes. To both, I mean. Questions, that is."

I was talking to the reflection. When I turned to speak to the voice, I couldn't. Speak, that is. I have never, in almost all my nearly 53 years seen such a stunning woman, and believe me I've seen a few. This female police person made Cindy Crawford look like Quasimodo's twin sister.

"Allow me, *m'sieur*." She pushed the door open effortlessly and brushed past me. "Please to come in. I help you, wizz ze French perhaps?"

The kind of French she had in mind bore no resemblance to the French I had in mind, but I said 'yes' anyway and followed her in.

The thought of being arrested for drunken, reckless driving and

5

causing GBH to a noble medieval doorstep had suddenly turned from one of abject terror to a delight many people would pay good money for — lots of it.

The interview lasted only 15 minutes, far too short for my liking. I'd have happily stayed all day.

All fear of police, uniforms and guns had gone. As far as they were concerned, all I'd done was park the hire car where I shouldn't have. They gave me a ticket, then forgot to ask me for the fine and the lovely police lady showed me to the door and took me to the car pound. I paid the £50 towing charge gladly.

"You really should be in the movies, y'know," I said, tucking the receipt into my wallet. I know, it's an old line. She smiled, but that was all. "I'm a producer. Attending the *Forum Cartoon*, at Latitudes. You know where that is?"

"Yes, *m'sieur*. Eet's a long way from ze town. How you get there now? Ze car, ees not to drive, ees eet?"

I hadn't looked too closely at the poor thing the night before. I was too busy legging it.

The front wheel just hung limply at a curious angle, the tyre had been torn to shreds, presumably by the bumper which was buckled at an angle of 90 degrees.

"No. The hire company are getting me a replacement. I must go back to the hotel." I paused and gazed into her gorgeous blue eyes. "What time do you knock off?"

"Knock off? What ees this 'knock off'?"

"Er sorry. Finish work, I mean."

"Oh, at two o'clock. Why you ask?"

"I was thinking dinner perhaps, tonight. I'd be very grateful. I need an interpreter. I'm trying to do a deal with a French company, from Paris, and they don't speak very good English."

Always was quick thinking, me.

"Zat would be very nice. Should I come to your hotel, L'Forum isn't eet?"

She'd remembered! I'd had to give my hotel address to the policeman who'd taken my details and she'd remembered. I was on.

6

"Yes. Around eight o'clock. That OK?"

"Yes, m'sieur. Eight o'clock then. I am Brigitte."

She held her right hand out and I shook it.

"Brigitte. Call me Peter, please."

"Peetair. Of course. Until then."

She turned and I watched the hips sway back towards the police station. I couldn't believe my luck. All I had to do now was find some French speaking idiots to pose as a Paris production company and complete the charade. Not easy. Walking back towards the hotel I was suddenly hit with inspiration. They wouldn't turn up and I'd have to take her out for dinner anyway. Just the two of us. Brilliant!

"Nimes airport? How far is that from Arles?"

"About twenty kilometres, m'sieur. You can go there now. A car waits for you."

The lady from Europe Assist was still a tad icy, but helpful anyway. I put the phone down and made my way downstairs to reception and the palatial front entrance of the hotel.

The previous day I'd seen various gliteratti from the *Forum Cartoon* coming and going in a huge stretch-out Mercedes limo. Outside the Hotel l'Forum it was waiting for me. The driver jumped out and held one of many doors open.

"M'sieur. For Nimes airport?"

"Yes. That's me."

I got in and enjoyed the air-conditioning for the next twenty minutes. Didn't cost me a bean. Europe Assist footed the bill, the driver explained. All I had to do was sign the chitty.

A few formalities later, completed at the Lo-Cost Rent-a-Car desk inside the airport concourse, and I went to find the almost new Renault Safrane in the car park. Bloody loonies, trusting me with an almost new Safrane. It had everything, air-conditioning included, and it was black. I'd purposely booked a Ford Fiesta because it was the cheapest I could get and it was small, ideal for the narrow streets. Sadly, the Fiesta was not narrow enough, it had proved. God knows how the Safrane would cope. I started up, familiarised myself with the few basic controls, then made for the exit. Trying to negotiate the car park exit, I had to reverse and re-position the car in order to get the token into the machine which raised the barrier. I felt a bump. Then heard an American voice.

"Hey! Hey! You just reversed right into my automobile!"

Fortunately there was no damage, but I drove nervously to Latitudes and went in through the back door.

"Hi, Pete. Got the car sorted?" asked Chris, after I'd located him in the lounge.

We went to the bar and ordered two coffees. I told him all about my adventures and Brigitte. He was mightily impressed, but disappointed. I think he was hoping for dinner with me that night, our last together in France.

"Sorry Chris, but this is important. She's a stunner. I can't believe my luck."

It didn't hold. My luck, that is.

Brigitte never showed and I did end up having dinner with Chris and the boys at the restaurant right opposite my hotel. I kept looking over towards the hotel entrance, but no. She never came and I went to bed on my own once again.

Chapter 2

LA BONNE IDÉE

*In which I discover Brouville and the lake,
meet my friendly French café patron François
and plan my chartering idea.*

When planning my trip to Provence I'd purchased 'The
Rough Guide', highly recommended by the lady in my local
bookshop in Macclesfield, Cheshire, the old home town. I read it
avidly and planned my next few days around a strict itinerary.
You have to have a plan.

The day after my lonely, disappointing night in Arles I set off for
Fontaine-de-Vaucluse via Les Baux and the Cathederale d'Images.
'The Rough Guide' extolled the virtues of Fontaine, so I'd set my
mind on staying a night there. What a dump. Sure enough, as 'The
Rough Guide' pointed out, there were lots of museums in
Fontaine. It didn't tell me that there were also two thousand of the
world's great unwashed. All sucking ice cream or gobbling slices
of evil smelling pizza, as they wandered from museum to
museum.

Les Baux, on the other hand, had been described as a rip-off,
'Everywhere you go in Les Baux, you get the feeling you're being
ripped-off', it said. I didn't. The place is stunning, a citadel sitting
high on a rocky escarpment, eerie and spooky. And an excellent
plat-du-jour set me back just £8, including two beers. The
Cathedrale d'Images, just down the road, is also a place I would
recommend to anybody visiting Provence. A disused bauxite
mine (yes, *baux*ite! Get it?) has been turned into a subterranean
audio-visual experience you just cannot describe. So I shan't try.

I was beginning to consider 'The Rough Guide' in a different
light.

Reading between the lines, I left Fontaine and headed for L'Isles.
Accommodation was secured at Le Hotel le Bassin and I took
advantage of *le douche* after le hot, sticky day sightseeing.

Picking up 'The Rough Guide', I discovered that the trout served in the restaurant of Le Bassin was 'good value'. It was. They got that right. But by now I was starting to change my itinerary. Most of that evening was spent thumbing through 'The Rough Guide' and earmarking places they slagged off as a must to visit. One such is Pruniers, a little town at the northern end of a huge lake called Le Lac de Ste Serre and not far from the Gorges du Durance. In 'The Rough Guide', Pruniers is described as 'one place to avoid — a bit of a sham'. I found it enchanting, a village reminiscent of Portmerion, very stylish and up-market.

And then, at the southern end of Le Lac I found Brouville, not mentioned in 'The Rough Guide', and the place I'm going to devote the rest of this tome to.

It doesn't take long to wander around Brouville, something like 60 houses, a church and a school with the usual few basic shops, an *auberge*, post office and *bar tabac*, as well as a few other bars and cafés. I'd done my wander, noted that the village boasted a *Club Nautique* and sat down on a lakeside bar terrace and ordered coffee. It was mid-morning and warm and sunny.

I was enjoying the late September sun and gazed longingly at the greeny-blue waters of the lake, 20 yards away across the road and day-dreamed of yottin' here. I'd stayed the previous night in Seyne, a small town some 15 kilometres from the lake, but from what I'd seen on my journey from Pruniers, I'd decided to return and explore the lake surrounds some more. A permanent life in Provence would have to include close proximity to water.

When the chap returned with my coffee, I asked for a *croissant* and was told to go to the *boulangerie* next door. I liked the style of the chap — he could've gone himself and made a small profit, but no. I went off and purchased my DIY breakfast. The lady in the *boulangerie* was ear-marked for another visit and I returned to the cafe to partake of aforementioned breakfast. I gathered that the chap in the cafe was closing down and I enquired why. The tourists had all gone home, he said. That was that. The season was over and he had had enough. I was his last customer of 1997.

I finished my breakfast and walked around to the *auberge* to see if they'd closed down as well. I was in luck. Still open and they had a room for the night. I checked in, the tour of Provence had come to a temporary halt.

"Zere are no snobbish in Brouville, you unnerstan whar-I-mean?"

"Yes. I unnerstan, Francois."

It's hard to describe my relationship with François, suffice to say that, in the space of 24 hours we became the firmest of friends.

There are some people you click with straight away and François is one such. A dapper, moustachioed man, François has a smile for everyone, and rarely says anything bad about anybody, anybody that is who lives in Brouville. And he knows everybody who lives in Brouville. It's a small place and François' Cafe du Soleil is right in the middle of Brouville. And Brouville is the place I had decided to live in, possibly forever.

Never mind women, I'd fallen in love with a village.

François' comment about the populace of the village is a very accurate one. I spoke with quite a few in my two days there.

Mr Goodbody is a retired orthopaedic surgeon and an excellent if somewhat unorthodox *boules* player. Reggie, as he insists on being called, told me that he came to Brouville by mistake, much as I had. That was thirty years ago. He decided that this was where he wanted to end his days, so he bought his cottage opposite the Café du Soleil, adjacent to the *boules* pitch and with a magnificent view of the setting sun over the lake. He showed me round the cottage and introduced me to his wife. I've rarely met such wonderful people. I hope they live forever.

I suppose that looking for somewhere to live was my primary reason for going to Provence. It's all Peter Mayle's fault. I blamed being there on the doorstep, but in truth, I should blame Peter Mayle. Having read his 'A Year in Provence' several times, it's hard to describe just what he's done to me. A subliminal thought train has been in the back of my mind since first picking the damn book up.

11

And here I was, sitting outside the Café du Soleil with François, planning the rest of my life .

"Zey are too much, ze houses in Brouville."

"Never mind the houses, François. This village is too much."

"You want to buy Brouville?!"

"No, you silly sausage. I mean it's just perfect — too much. It's an English expression for something that's perfect, the best — or better than the best."

"Too much. Yes. Zat is Brouville."

He chuckled, the very French chuckle that involves a lot of shoulder wobbling and holding the arms apart. I love François.

"Trouble is I don't think I can afford it, buying a house I mean. But I did have an idea last night. See what you think of this."

I told him my idea.

Rent out my cottage in England, take my yacht to Brouville, drop it in the lake, tie it to the municipal pontoon and do day charters for the grockles. I could live on the yacht and make enough to live on. *Une Bonne Idée* if ever there was one, and a chance to get to know the place and the people before making any decision about putting down more permanent roots.

"Go for eet, Peetair. Go for eet. Brilliant. Zere is nobody doing zis thing. You will clear off."

"I hope you mean clean up!"

The chuckle again.

"Yes. Clean up. Zis is what I mean."

So that was that, for the moment.

La Bonne Idée had been conceived and the gestation period had begun.

The next morning I bade farewell to Brouville and François, promising to keep in touch with him as progress was made with *La Bonne Idée*, and headed back towards Nice airport, via Cannes.

I really did have a warm feeling towards Provence, but felt I should take in a bit of the coast and could think of nowhere finer to do so than the capital of film festivals and yottin'. As I drove down the promenade I spied several very large and classic looking yachts all milling around and looking for all the world as if they were about to start a race. I parked the hire car and taking my camera, made my way down to the end of the breakwater which protects the harbour from the worst of the Mediterranean swell. The yachts were indeed starting a race, the *Noilarge*, a race from Cannes, around a rock off north Corsica and back. It was spectacular to watch the start, as the cream of the world's classic racing yachts jostled for position and approached the start line. I took many snaps and thought of my good yottie pal Gaz, who is one of the very best at yott-spottin'. He'd be so jealous when he saw my piccies. The yachts left for Corsica and I left for the airport.

The Renault arrived there safely and I followed the young Lo-Cost Rent-a-Car lady around as she inspected the car for damage. Satisfied that I'd not put a scratch on it, she asked for all my paperwork and informed me that I would be charged the 1500FF (£150) insurance excess for the damage to the Fiesta.

All in all, it was a very relieved Marsh who settled back in his seat and took off for Luton, but all that was to change some two months later when I tried to pay for a tankful of petrol with my Visa, and it was refused. Telephoning them, I was informed that the sum of £4163 had been taken from my account by Lo-Cost, Nice, and my credit limit was only £1600.

That started a long, drawn-out dispute which was to cause much anxiety and, as the tale unfolds, you will learn more, dear reader.

Chapter 3

A RIP-RAPPING YARN

In which I introduce you to my close yottin'
buddies and son Luke, buy and re-fit my yacht
Rip-Rap and go for an action-packed
maiden solo voyage.

A laconic Frenchman sauntered past the Café, an evil-smelling, yellow *mais* Gitanes clamped firmly between his thin, mean lips, his black eyebrows and moustache both knitted individually and yet seemingly together in a determined frown. The careworn leather pouch containing his *boules* dangled beside his bronzed and extremely hirsute knees, and his flip-flops flipped and flopped.

I find that life is full of imponderables and the sound that flip-flops make is one of them. I picked up the glass from the white-topped, umbrella shaded table and sipped my *pastis*. The ice was quickly melting. It was late September and early evening, yet Brouville was still warm and looking more and more attractive as a potential place to put down roots. François had returned to the kitchen and was preparing my steak and all I could think of was a future home for myself and my beloved yacht.

The village of Brouville nestles on a hillside overlooking its own lagoon, a spur off the south eastern corner of the lake itself. It's narrow here, opposite the Café, and I watched as a single sailboat, an Enterprise dinghy, tacked its way back up the lagoon and towards the pontoon, just around the corner and out of my sight in a natural wind shadow, a sheltered place if ever there was one. This night, what wind there was came from the south east and made the lagoon easy to get out of, that little bit harder to get back into. I imagined myself there on my yacht, tacking back in after an afternoon's yottin' which would have included some general merriment and mirth with a few friends, the pinky-red setting sun on our backs, and sighed. I was daydreaming; back to imponderables.

14

How is it possible that two identically machine-formed pieces of rubber footwear hitting two almost identically formed pieces of the human anatomy can make two completely different sounds? And why 'flip-flop' and not 'flop-flip'? I must ask Duncan, I thought, he'll know.

Duncan is a fellow yottie, he and I have sailed together for some years and the previous year, completely unknown to each other, we had both purchased two almost identical yachts and our moorings were almost within hailing distance of each other on the Menai Straits. Many weekends were spent sailing in company and exploring the North Wales coast together on my Friendship 22, 'Rip-Rap', and Duncan's Hunter Duette, 'Rufus'. The airwaves crackled with 'Rufus, Rufus, Rufus. This is Rip-Rap, Rip-Rap, Rip-Rap. Come in please'.

In order to turn a coin Duncan is the titular leader of the Department of Podiatry at Salford University, Head Podiatrist, I suppose — 'boss biffter footquack' to you and I — so chances are I thought, as the flip-flopping *boules* player turned a corner and disappeared from view, he'll know the answer to that one.

Dunc is a small but jovial fellow, much given to mirth and good ideas, most of which seem to happen without him being there. But that's Duncan and without his tremendous enthusiasm for life, the world would be a lonelier place. Incidentally, he once told me the story of the two dyslexic skiers, one night sipping whisky at anchor, after a good day's yott and an ale-warmed evening in the Ty Coch at Porth Dinlleyn.

"Excuse me," says one of the dyslexic skiers to a passing stranger with a sledge under his arm. "I wonder if you could help settle an argument. My friend and I have just descended the piste and we can't agree on whether we have been performing zig-zigs or zag-zags."

"No good asking me chum," comes the reply. "I'm a tobogganist."

"Oh." The skier sounded disappointed. But he added, with a brighter tone of voice, "Well, in that case, could we have 20 Bensons?"

I fell about laughing and told this joke to my son, Luke. He's dyslexic and enjoyed it too.

I ramble on about these things for a very good reason — the name of my boat.

I'm often asked, 'Why Rip-Rap?' Could have been 'Flip-Flop', 'Zig-Zig', 'Zag-Zag' or even 'Zig-Zag', all good names for a thing that floats and performs extraordinary water-borne manoeuvres. To be truthful, I couldn't pronounce the original name, let alone spell it. The previous owner had explained to me that it was a Zulu word meaning 'little ray of sunshine'. Yuk!! Macho Marsh floating around on a little ray of sunshine? Sorry, just not me. And I could well imagine getting into a spot of bother and having to spell it several times over the radio to the Holyhead Coastguard. Didn't bear thinking about.

Also, when I was carrying out some re-fitting at the boatyard where she lay at the time of purchase, I remember the girls in the chandlery sighing with relief whilst writing her new name on the purchase orders.

"Thank God," one said.

But that's not what Duncan said.

"You can't do that, old boy! It's dashed bad luck, changing the name of a boat."

"You're talking a load of twaddle, Dunc," I said. "Old fishermen's yarns. Poppycock. Anyway, loads of boats have had their names changed and nothing much has happened to them. 'Maiden', for instance. Storming success for the girlies."

Dunc was not to be persuaded, it's bad luck and that's that. And besides, he could be right. Read on.

As a callow, spotty youth, I derived much pleasure from setting off those deadly, jumping fireworks next to girls' legs (they wore skirts on Bonfire Night in those days). The resultant efforts of these potential transports of delight to get away from my evil-doing gave me hours of masochistic mirth and, as they fell into my arms trying to avoid the damn things, provided a launch pad to some memorable gropes around the back of sheds and things.

So, as my intentions were that my new found toy, something of a firework in itself judging by family reaction to the purchase, would have a similar effect on the available members of the female persuasion 40 years on, Rip-Rap it is. I'll grow up one day.

As previously mentioned, Rip-Rap is a Friendship 22, a Dutch built trailer-sailer, 4-berth, roller-reefing, lazy jacks, an adequate sail wardrobe, and equally adequate instrumentation, but with the added advantage of a Hostess trolley, as my mate Gaz calls it. It was Gaz who'd pointed her out to me as we wandered through the boatyard dismissing one disappointment after another.

A few days earlier I'd rung him and invited myself down for a weekend on his yacht, 'Hunca Munca'. The intention was, I'd told him, for me to look at likely vessels, Marsh for the use of. He'd spotted one or two and arranged for me to see inside them. Total disappointment. Not one I even remotely liked. So here we were gazing at the prettiest little sloop I've laid eyes on and Gaz is saying:

"Think you'd better get the keys for this one, Pete."

I knew I couldn't afford her, she must be well out of my budget, I thought, but what the hell, the keys were got and we were sitting in the cabin. I couldn't take the grin off my face, Gaz could tell I was sold on her. Then my grin disappeared.

"Hang on a mo, Gaz — where do you cook?"

"Pull that handle over there," he says. So I does.

Crafty sod. He'd been on a Friendship before. Told me he knew two lads in Liverpool who'd raced one and they were mightily impressed with the performance. Had to remove the Hostess though. It weighs a ton.

The Hostess is a very neatly designed sliding galley (a kitchen unit comprising cooker, sink and utensil storage) which disappears from view when not in use — a feature which actually sold me on the vessel.

I went to the brokerage and put in an offer, way over budget, but, as mentioned before, what the hell. If I was successful there'd be some careful negotiating to do with the bank, building society or whoever. Gaz and I repaired to The Union Inn for copious ales and inducement of a general feeling of well-being. The chap behind the bar bored Gaz stiff with stories of the sea, the

'Conway' going aground in the Swellies and how he'd been up the Amazon on a tanker. Me, I couldn't care less. He could've been up the Orinoco without a certain instrument as far as I was concerned.

I owned a yacht and I was already thinking of names and designs for the T-shirts.

For some years I'd cruised with Gaz on Hunca Munca, an Evolution 26, but once a year, Gaz, Dunc, Tim, another pal who will shortly appear in this yarn, and myself, would enter the Puffin Island Race, a short dash half way round Anglesey. In 1991, our first attempt, we'd finished a highly creditable 6th and when 1992 came I had some extremely kitsch polo shirts embroidered with the yacht's namestyle, 'Hunca Munca' and 'Puffin Island Race 1992'. I did not want to tempt fate and add 'Winners' to the design, but after the race, as I doled out the shirts to the boys whilst we prepared to go ashore to Holyhead Sailing Club, we felt very confident. On handicap, we reckoned we'd trounced the opposition. The accolade was surely ours.

It had all really happened off Carmel Head, in between the Skerries and the most northerly tip of Anglesey.

We'd had a fairly uneventful sail up until then; Dunc, Tim and I sat on the rail and kept Hunca Munca as flat as we could whilst Gaz wiggled the stick and chuntered. He chunters a lot, Gaz, when he's yottin'. I think it helps to keep his concentration up, but occasionally it serves to vent his anger on one or all of the crew. Let's face it, we can all make mistakes and I'm not one to hide when I've made one. Gaz is. Somehow, it's never his fault. It doesn't enter into his pysche.

To relieve the tension Dunc passed round a soggy paper bag with some Danish pastries in and that shut him up for a while. Loves his scram does Gaz. Anyway, there we were doing really quite well when suddenly Gaz let out a shriek, a shriek partially muffled by half a mouthful of Danish pastry.

"Where's that bloody Scampy come from?"

I looked down at my Danish pastry and gingerly peeled it open.

No scampi in mine. I turned to Tim.

"You got scampi?"

But he wasn't listening. All three were staring at a mean looking racer sneaking up inside us. A red hull, with a white flash of lightning painted along the side — a formidable sight and apparently a Scampy. Another, even more formidable sight met my eyes — Lucifer himself.

Dark, close and deep set eyes, the mass of black close-cropped curls forming a widow's peak on his forehead. Only the horns weren't there, visibly to us humans, but I knew better. Unmistakable. It was Adrian. He stood in the cockpit, right at the back, quietly but firmly giving orders to the crew as they quickly and efficiently put in a rapid tack. We were doomed. I've sailed the Atlantic with Adrian and I can tell you, he's a mean yottie.

"Hi, Ade. How y're doin'." I waved in a vain attempt to distract him.

He just waved back with a smile and ordered another tack.

"Ready about!" Gaz was galvanised into action and I could tell he didn't want one of his crew fraternising with the opposition.

Tim, Dunc and I descended into the cockpit and took our positions.

"Ready."

"Ready."

"Ready."

We were ready. But not ready for what was to turn out to be the longest and most exhausting tacking duel I've ever been involved in. Forty five minutes and fifty seven tacks later, I died — metaphorically. I might just as well have been dead, the amount of use I was going to be for the rest of the race.

By this time the wind had got up and we were headed out into Holyhead Bay. Gaz had decided we'd fought the tide and the Scampy long enough and it was a losing battle anyway.

"You know these tides, Pete. Gaz says tell us when to tack in towards the breakwater."

Tim, next to me on the rail, was speaking from a faraway land. Norway, perhaps, although it looked more like Greenland. I didn't reply, I couldn't. The efforts of the past hour, plus the fact that 50 percent of the time I was underwater made conversation a tad on the hard side.

'Green', it's called. When you're totally immersed in sea water, you see green. Used to be one of my favourite colours. Not any more. I saw enough green that afternoon to last me a lifetime.

"Now!"

It wasn't a structured, considered or informed tactical move, simply desperation. I'd had enough.

Enough green, enough wet, enough of seeing my Danish pastry again and again. I wanted to go home. It was my version of "Are we nearly there yet, Daddy?" and for some daft reason I thought it would be warmer and drier on the other side.

Gaz tacked. Tim and Dunc did the string pulling — it was only one tack after all. I rolled over the coachroof and stuck my weary legs under the guardrail.

Then I fell asleep.

Tim tells the rest of this story far better than I. After all, he was awake at the time. He first told it in Holyhead Sailing Club that night and he's been telling it ever since.

Like Duncan, Tim is imbued with a great natural enthusiasm for life, life in the fast lane.

A stocky man with naturally curly blonde hair, a square-jawed and craggy, yet smiley visage, only the laughter lines marking an otherwise remarkably unlined face. Tremendously fit, Tim throws himself at any challenge (he won his first ski race despite breaking a leg as he threw himself across the finish line) and another seriously good yacht racer. My son Luke, now seventeen, went sailing on Tim's yacht Black Dog, a lean, mean, stripped-out racing machine. It was the first time Luke had spent more than moments in company with Tim and afterwards he asked me what he did for a living.

I told him.

"Buys and sells second-hand Jaguars."

"Figures," was all Luke said, but that's Tim. A second-hand car dealer. Personally, I wouldn't have him any other way and, as Tim has made this story his own, I shall tell it as he does. You will gather, dear reader, from what I've told you thus far, it's way off being the truth.

"So there we were, bloody miles out in Holyhead Bay, wet, cold, knackered, and this bastard's fast asleep. Talk about cool! He'd shouted when to tack and fell asleep. Gaz couldn't stop chuntering. 'Silly bastard. We're sunk now. We'll never get this one back. We're dead meat. Wassock. Wait till we get into Holyhead. I'll kill him.' He never stopped, until we came up to the breakwater. One tack, bloody miles from anywhere, and he'd got it spot on. Right behind us was the Scampy. You should've seen their faces. We just came from nowhere. It didn't matter that they passed us then. We'd got ten or more minutes on them with handicap. It was ours. The dog's bollocks!"

As we four identically dressed, smug crewmen swaggered into the club and up to the bar, the OD (Chief Flag Officer of the Day) came over to me and said, with a grin,

"Sorry Pete, you guys were deemed over the line at the start. We've had to give you a ten minute penalty. Pity — you'd have won by around six minutes otherwise. Better luck next year."

What did the asshole mean, 'Deemed'?

What is deemed, what deemed, who fucking deemed, what constitutes a deem? Well, never mind. Fifth overall with a ten minute penalty. The best result to date. Surely it would be ours next year. We didn't say anything to Gaz who was on the helm at the start and was obviously in control of us being over the line, we just celebrated by deeming ourselves a pint of Guinness for each minute of the deemed penalty.

Gaz, Dunc and Tim are not the only people I've sailed with over the many years I've felt the pull of the sea. The rest are too many and varied to mention here, but one or two may crop up during the unravelling of this tale.

However, it is necessary now to mention one other who has escaped thus far the unholy wrath of Marsh — one Dave Mills, 'The Swimmer' to his pals. I met The Swimmer (he teaches swimming, incidentally) that evening in Holyhead Sailing Club.

He was with his wife Pauline and youngest daughter Sophie, who took the fancy of Marsh instantly. Thirty years' age difference is a nonce, in my mind anyway.

Sophie was entranced with my cigarette rolling machine, she thought I was constantly working out complex arithmetical theorems on a pocket calculator. In fact, I roll a fag just about every fifteen minutes when pouring copious ales down my throat, so she must have thought I was some kind of genius, being able to work out these things whilst getting seriously smashed. I digress. It's Big Daft Dave I was on about.

At that time Dave owned a Contessa 27, in fact one of the boats Gaz had singled out for me to view and reject. But last year the lovely Pauline bought him a Nicholson 31 called 'Trenarth', a magnificent ship of the line and destined to make Gaz so jealous he's gone and bought one too.

Trenarth made her first appearance, complete with the entire Mills family, at a most memorable beach Bar-B-Q in Pilot's Cove last August. Gaz was there with Hunca Munca and his boss, Nigel. On Rip-Rap, I had along Tim's lady of the moment, Janine, her son and a friend, Tim being on the other side of the Lleyn Peninsula that weekend contesting a Regatta. Duncan was nowhere to been seen, of course. It had been his idea, this gathering. For weeks he'd been ringing round rallying the troops and on the day, he wasn't there. But it gave vent to Big Dave's humour and he can be very, very funny. Even Janine, who didn't know Duncan, was in fits.

Dave was marching up and down the beach giving a mock speech, the kind you always hear at the end of a Regatta.

"I'd like to thank the OD for setting such interesting and varied courses, the Ladies Committee for providing us with the most interesting and varied menu, in several courses, but, most importantly I'd like to thank the Social Secretary, Duncan, for organising this event and, typically, not turning up. Hey, I'll tell you what, we ought to start some kind of joke club. It wouldn't half upset the Sailing Club members with all their jealous sniping at us lot. If only they could see us now!"

For some while we had been the butt of some pretty snidey

remarks from the stick-in-the-mud members of the dinghy racing club we all belong to. 'Imagine our off-shore friends sitting in their rain-soaked, wind-swept cockpits' was one remark published in the monthly bulletin. I suppose it was only harmless fun, but all the same, you could say there might have been a hint of jealousy creeping in there somewhere, and Dave was right. If only they could've seen us now, sitting or sprawling on the flat-topped rocks and golden sand which is Pilot's Cove, Llandryn Island, on the west coast of Anglesey. Tremendous humour abounded and the kebabs sizzled as copious ales were quaffed and the boats rode gently at anchor in the warm afternoon sun.

The West Anglesey Nautical Cruising Association was born that day on Pilot's Cove beach. More of that later.

Days after making my purchase bid for Rip-Rap, 'subject to survey', I received a phone call from the surveyor (I'd appointed a local chap on the broker's recommendation).

"She's rotten," he said. "The whole cabin is rotten!"

My heart leapt, stomach churned and I wanted her so badly. I was in love and the Hostess trolley looked pretty damned sound to me. A phone call to the brokers did my palpitations no good at all, somebody else had put in a higher bid!

"OK... I'll offer the asking price, subject to survey. Does that mean she's mine?"

I was dying inside — how could a body take so much emotion in such a short time? The voice on the other end of the telephone line was so calm, so laid-back, so assuring. But that's his job. He knew he'd got a sale, one way or the other.

"Of course, Mr Marsh."

A few days later I was sitting in Rip-Rap's cabin opposite the broker, studying the frown on his worried face. The surveyor's report was in my hand, the longest fax I've ever received.

Some people don't bother with surveys when buying a boat; Duncan's one of them ('You don't need to survey a Hunter, old boy!'), but I couldn't help feeling that this had been the best £160 I'd ever spent. Fastidious wasn't in it. And remember, I'd had the gist of it when I'd upped my offer to the asking price in order to secure the boat as mine. Now the price was about to come down to somewhere in the region of my initial offer, if I could swing it.

A copy of the main eight items on the surveyor's list were in the broker's hand and he'd dismissed all but one as being 'easy to handle'. That at least was true. Nothing that wasn't within the remit of a half-way competent DIY man. Then it came to the rotten cabin. It wasn't actually as bad as the surveyor had originally made out, all that really needed doing was the whole cabin structure taking out and replacing. At least, that's what I was holding out for.

The frown didn't disappear, it just eased a little.

"Well, we're looking at twelve to fifteen hundred, I reckon."

He looked up at me and smiled.

I thought of a cat I'd once owned. He used to look at me like that when he wanted feeding. The look was usually accompanied by a silky, pleading miaow. I smiled back.

"That's it then. Fifteen hundred off the asking price."

"A thousand? Perhaps?"

It wasn't a miaow, but it was damned close.

"Twelve fifty."

"I'll go and speak to the owner."

And with that he got up and went back to his office. I was left on my own, sitting in the cabin I was to get to know so well and smiling ruefully to myself. I have an extraordinary pal called Roger, an ex-MI5 man and a master chippie, who'd eat this job for breakfast. What the broker had given me was a quote for the boatyard to carry out the work. If all went to plan I'd jump in the car, drive back to Macclesfield, find Roger in one of his four regular haunts and make him an offer, the sort of offer I knew Roge just couldn't refuse.

"OK. She's yours." The broker's face was poking through the hatchway and I felt like kissing it. "I'll draw up the paperwork now."

Yowser!

"Just keep me fed and watered. I've told you. It'll be a bit of a break for me and my little petal. She'll be glad to get rid of me."

Roge never did take much persuading, and this time was no exception. He'd do my job at weekends, for food and drink, as long as I paid for the materials. We could sleep on the boat to save B&B costs and the way I'd described the job, Roge reckoned three weekends, top side. It was to take four, but I'll come to that in a while.

To begin to describe Roge is difficult — but I'll try. I've said before about him being in MI5, that part's true. He has told me some tales but I'm a bit loathe to air them in public. Suffice to say that they beggar belief. So in order for you to grasp a little of the character of the man, what I will tell you is the well documented story of how Roge spent his mother's inheritance. I say well documented, but I don't know if anyone has actually put it down in writing before. I know it's well discussed in the pubs around Macclesfield and I've heard it from many different sources, so I guess it's true.

Roge's dad was a master builder and taught his son everything he knows. Roge has just fine-tuned his father's skills and, as a result, has become an extremely talented and thorough craftsman. The only thing he won't do is painting and decorating.

"You'll never catch me with a brush in me 'and," he once said, but I have, once — and I've got the photo to prove it. To be fair he wasn't painting, rather putting preservative on some untreated wood, but he had a brush in his hand and to me, that counts.

His father died when Roge was in his twenties and he left Roge's mum fairly comfortably off, not rich, but comfortable. Mrs Bowyer loved her only son but wouldn't have anything to do with him. Roge's drinking habits were in complete disharmony with her strict Methodist upbringing and ultimately those same habits found disfavour with the Secret Service. Roger got out. Whether he was pushed or fell, we'll never know. He returned to Macclesfield and the building trade, a way of life more suited to the Bowyer mentality.

It came as something of a surprise therefore when Roge was called to his mother's solicitor's office and told of the relative fortune she'd left him. I say 'relative' because for years Roge has lived hand-to-mouth — literally, and still does. He's happy if he earns enough money in a day to pay for the beer that's going down his neck that night. He wakes up penniless and starts over. However, the way in which he was to treat what relatives he did have left is a mark of the man.

His ex-wife and two daughters got a house each and his son a brand new red Porsche. That was his 'relative' duty done. Then he went to Leek to visit a friend who owned a pub. It was market day and the pubs stayed open all afternoon (these were the days of prohibition). Around three o'clock Roge realised he didn't have enough money to last him through, so he went to the bank and said 'I want some money.' A perfectly normal thing to do, but Roge didn't have a chequebook, a credit card or any form of ID. He was also dressed as if he'd just come off a building site (in fairness he had, two or three weeks before). He can also have a threatening manner can Roger.

He's tall and lean, weathered and scarred, with only three fingers on his left hand. He loves telling the story of how he lost the forefinger, when a circular saw caught on something and went out of control, completely severing the finger and working its way up his forearm, and my bottom always goes funny.

He leant on the counter of the bank and stared at the girl behind the glass, gently stroking his stubbled chin with his three-fingered left hand.

"Just ring the NatWest in Macc," he said as politely as possible to the girl behind the glass. "Tell 'em Roger Bowyer wants some money."

She rang, somewhat apologetically returned and said,

"That seems to be in order. How much, Mr Bowyer?"

"Just start counting. I'll tell you when to stop."

I don't know how much he drew out but Roger left the bank ten minutes later and returned to his friend's pub.

A good afternoon was had by all and some time during the early evening a cab was ordered to take a somewhat inebriated Mr Bowyer back home to Macclesfield. He never made home, not that night anyway. He ordered the cab driver to stop at one of his haunts and told him to wait. A few minutes later he emerged from the pub with a very attractive if rather blowsy young lady called Michelle.

Now don't misunderstand, Michelle is not a lady of the night. I know, I've met her. She has a heart of gold and a diesel-powered repartee. You know where you are with Michelle. And Michelle knew just where she was that night. What she didn't know is where she was going.

The person I feel sorriest for in this somewhat bizarre tale is the cabbie. He lost his job, his wife kicked him out and, as far as anyone knows, he's never been seen since. The reason, dear reader, is this.

"Take us to Scotland. I want to do some fishing."

"Scotland! D'you know how much that's going to cost?" said the incredulous cabbie.

"Look. Here's fifteen hundred quid. Tell us when you need more."

And that was the start of quite an adventure. For the next ten days the cab zig-zagged across Scotland in a series of mishaps, misdoings and malt-induced mayhem that made Della and the Dealer and the dog named Boo look like monastic morons. Tom Sharpe would've had difficulty thinking this one up.

Roge and Michelle survived if the cabbie didn't, and for one I'm grateful, for Roge anyway. Michelle can without doubt look after herself.

"Like I said, three weekends. Top side."

The boat was in Bangor, but we were in Menai Bridge. The Mostyn Arms, Menai Bridge, to be precise.

We were here in order to discuss the job which we'd just given what Roge described as 'a dose of looking at' and for me to put a face to a name, one John Owen, Piermaster.

I had purchased The Swimmer's mooring tackle, as Trenarth was going to need something considerably more substantial than the one he'd used for the Contessa, and had been allocated a location by Ynys Mon, the Isle of Anglesey Council. It was opposite Menai pier but, by definition, across the Straits. And that meant across one of the fiercest tidal rips in British coastal waters. The thought of launching myself over that lot with a few pints on board and nothing more than a flimsy piece of inflatable rubber between me and Davy Jones was, to put it mildly, terrifying. I was hoping to persuade Owen the Pier to re-locate me slightly nearer to the only two decent pubs on that part of the Straits and so I'd rung him the previous day and learned that he would be in The Mostyn that afternoon as there was 'some sort of rrr-ugby match on the telly, isn't it'.

Some sort of rugby match it turned out to be. England thrashed Wales in the Five Nations and Roge and I decided that it was perhaps a tad imprudent to try and persuade the rather large and more florid than usual Piermaster to alter his thinking on the mooring re-location idea. We had a few to celebrate the England victory though, quietly in the back bar, when the locals had silently gone home to their womenfolk. Then Gaz and The Swimmer turned up, so we had a few more and went for a curry. Afterwards we repaired to my boat — there was a bottle of whisky on board. 'Was' became the operative word.

The next day got off to a slow start, but by opening time Roge had worked out a way to make a drawbridge straight from the back of the boat to the back door of The Union Inn. That would save a lot of time and wasted effort walking the few hundred yards through the boatyard and up the back lane. To celebrate his ingenuity we did the walk. So that was one weekend gone.

I don't want to give you the wrong impression dear reader — I'm not an alcoholic, but I've been in the company of some fairly serious drinkers all through my adult life and I do find the pull of the public house extremely appealing. The banter and camaraderie that exists, together with the fact that the great British pub is a clearing house for all sorts of business, official, but largely unofficial, is what gives it appeal, to me anyway. I have always believed in buying at the right price rather than the right time. Rip-Rap was one such purchase. The fact that the deal wasn't done in a pub irks one slightly, but I could see the back wall of The Union over the broker's shoulder when he told me that she was mine.

The next three weekends quite honestly flew by.
Roger did his usual high quality job, stripping out all the rotten

timber and replacing it, and I stood by my end of the bargain, feeding and watering him — we'll draw a veil over the actual cost, suffice to say I didn't save too much on the broker's quote.

The chandlery bill was settled and a date was fixed for the launch.

My mother and son Luke had expressed extreme interest in being there for this most auspicious occasion and I'd booked a hotel room for Mother. Luke and I would spend our first night afloat on our own boat. The day, however, dawned slightly different to those in fairy stories.

I'd slept on board the previous night and had two more jobs to do before she went in the oggie. The self-adhesive name decals (I'd designed them myself in a typestyle which resembled dripping blood, apposite in the extreme, as you will learn) and the equally self-adhesive waterline stripes were to be affixed. The day had other ideas. A Force 8 gale and horizontal lashing rain made it damned near impossible, but I tried anyway. The name decals were fairly easy, but the waterline stripe went every which way.

"Oh, she looks wonderful, darling," was Mother's first exclamation as she and Luke climbed out of the car and came over to where I was applying the last few feet of stripe.

The second exclamation caused me to consider matricide.

"Are you going to re-do the other side as well, dear? It's rather wobbly."

I shall not repeat my reply, simply leave it to your imagination.

There have been many times in my life when I have tempted fate but that day wasn't going to be one of them. That was what I had decided, fate decided otherwise.

I'd had a word with the lads who operated the travel hoist and we'd jointly agreed that it was too wild and windy for the launch so we postponed. Mother was disappointed but suggested that we go for a pub lunch anyway. She knows her son!

A pub lunch was had and Mother and son said they'd go to the hotel and come back later. I went back to the boatyard. The rain had stopped and the wind abated. The travel hoist boys were busy launching and I was told that Rip-Rap was next. Panic! No time to go to the hotel, I just had to get on with it. Ten minutes later she was afloat.

We tied her to the dock wall starboard side on, where I was told she'd be protected from the wind if it got up again, but she'd dry out. That was OK if I stayed with her and made sure she settled against the wall. One very important lesson was learned that day. Never let Rip-Rap dry out starboard side on. The Hostess is on the port side.

Dry out she did, with me standing on the starboard side deck. A kind lady had put her ladder down the wall and onto the deck to allow me to climb off when I was ready to and then suddenly, there was a lurch.

I have a mortal fear of ladders, heights of any kind to be truthful. All the other kids in our neighbourhood used to climb trees. I stayed on terra firma. If anything I empathised with the mole family. I went up that ladder like a scalded cat and stood watching in abject horror as Rip-Rap put her mooring lines to the severest test they'd ever experienced. The mast was saved from being crumpled against the opposite dock wall by a matter of inches as she lay at 45 degrees and quivered.

"Where is she, dear?"

Mother stood beside me, but was staring fixedly ahead. I was looking down.

"There," I said.

Mother followed my worried gaze and looked down.

"Oh. She looks quite different from up here. And why is she leaning over at that funny angle?"

I tried to explain, but I don't think she fully understood. Luke said that he didn't think it would be a very good idea to sleep aboard that night and was mightily pleased when I agreed. We repaired to The Union where I booked a twin-bedded room with TV, which kept Luke happy, whilst I worried about what I might find in the dock the next morning.

One of the great things about being a dad is having a son to share things with. You know, macho things like drinking, womanising and yottin'.

For years the family holiday had been taken in Gwynedd during

Dinghy Week. I'd race my ageing 505 dinghy all morning, do the family bit in the afternoon and drink in the evening. That was until the ex-Mrs Marsh, *Accommodationkommandant*, discovered Rydd-y-Benllech, which must be the only village in Wales that doesn't have a pub (it used to, but it's an old folks' home now). It was bad enough to try and get through a Sunday on our family holidays in 'dry' Gwynedd, but then I was forced to get through a whole week in a rented cottage with the nearest pub being in Barmouth, a twenty-five minute walk away.

But then I got to enjoy walking and the evening constitutional became part of holiday life for the titular head of the Marsh family. I also discovered that Barmouth Yacht Club had a bar that opened on Sundays and they were obliged to serve visiting yachtsmen. The fact that my yacht was an ageing dinghy on a beach twenty miles away was one of those facts I felt the elders of BYC could usefully do without knowing.

When he was old enough to take an interest, Luke would join me in the racing bit, the 505 had gone and been replaced by an equally aged Mirror, a much more family-friendly craft. He'd also join me in the drinking bit during the evening as well, sometimes. I will never forget till the day I drop taking a two-year old, rather sick Luke into a fortunately empty pub and asking the kindly landlord if this was in order.

"Sure," he said, "as long as he's good."

Now kids I find, when they are genuinely ill are as good as gold and Luke was no exception. I propped him up in a corner and ordered a pint of beer and an orange squash. I took a large draught of the tawny foaming stuff and Luke did the same with his orange. With both hands, he placed his glass gently on the table and announced,

"This is nice pub, Daddy." Then he promptly threw up all over himself, the table, seat and carpet. "Oops, sorry Dad," he added.

I could've been seriously embarrassed, but fortunately the landlord had popped into the back room for something and hadn't noticed. I dashed to the gents, took a huge wodge of toilet paper, dashed back and had the mess cleaned up by the time he returned. I smiled and said,

"Lovely day."

"Yes," replied the landlord, but I could see his nostrils flaring at the rather unusual odour.

Shortly after the ex and I had split up, Luke and I spent a weekend with Gaz and his then partner's son Paul on Hunca Munca.

We rendezvous-ed at the Liverpool Arms in Menai on the Friday night and partook of some yottie scram. They do a gammon and eggs at the Liddy Arms you wouldn't believe, 'Death by Pig', I call it. Afterwards, a few pints were in order but this didn't appeal much to the boys, Luke then 13 and Paul 17, so they opted to go to the boat. Paul said he'd sit in the cockpit and wait for our signal, then come and fetch us in the dinghy. Highly appealing youngster was Paul.

By the time chucking out came Gaz and I had made a manful effort to drink the place dry and we meandered down to the pier. Gaz took out his torch and started flashing in the general direction of his mooring. Nothing, no sign of life whatsoever.

"What are the wassocks doing, for Christ's sake? Come on Paul. Dozy Dumbo's probably asleep," and other angry retorts were hurled across the water, but to no avail. The wind had got up and was blowing straight at us.

Then I noticed that Gazzer's torch wasn't actually flashing. The batteries were flat, or to be more precise, there weren't any batteries in it.

"Bugger," said Gaz, "knew there was something I'd forgotten to do."

That's the nearest I'd ever heard Gaz to admitting that he's been in the wrong. We returned to the cars and decided to bed down there for the night.

I didn't sleep much. Sleeping in cars has never appealed to me and I couldn't take my mind off Lukey. I hoped he was all right. God, if anything had happened to him I'd never forgive myself and incurring the wrath of the soon to be ex-Mrs Marsh was a painful threat. But then, in the cold, grey light of a Menai morning, we saw Hunca Munca slowly motoring up towards the pier and there on the foredeck, boathook in hand was the familiar figure of my son and heir. Relief!

They tied expertly up and Luke came ashore.
"Hi, Dad. You OK? We were worried about you."
He was worried about me. God bless him, he'll never know.

It was the sound of very, very powerful engines that woke me from a deep and dreamless slumber. That, and somebody shouting.

I climbed out of my bunk and stuck my head out of the hatch. Rip-Rap was bouncing around like a cork and a big wave suddenly hit her. I cracked my head a pearler and fell down the companionway. When I'd recovered and shaken my head a bit, I decided to have another go at determining if what I had seen was indeed the off-shore Moelfre lifeboat with full crew. It was.

The previous evening had been pleasantly spent with a couple of rather far-back but amusing gentleladies who numbered 'eventing' amongst their various pursuits. It was an 'event' that they were returning from and they'd decided to stop at The Moelfre Arms in order to purchase sustenance before journeying on.

"So you're a yottie, eh," said the obvious leader.

All pairs of women with sensible shoes have a leader and a lackey, I find.

"Yes," I replied, puffing myself up and waiting with great expectancy for the next question.

Go on, woman, ask me. Please!!

"And where is your yacht?"

Thank you, God.

"There, the white one with the dark blue stripes."

Yes!! They both gazed out of the mock Georgian bow-front window and down towards the calm of Moelfre Bay at Rip-Rap, gently riding at anchor in the glowing evening sun. It was quite a picture and I nearly cried with emotion just looking at her.

It was my first solo sail and destined to be one of the most memorable.

I'd had my maiden sail to Conway with Gaz the weekend before, then brought Rip-Rap back to the Straits with Tim the previous day and he'd gone back home, a woman in the offing, no doubt.

I stayed over and the next morning dawned so bright I decided to set sail for Amlwch. The Anglesey Pilot and tide tables were studied and a departure time from my mooring at Menai was set. I had a leisurely breakfast and set sail.

It was a super yott down the Straits past Beaumaris and through Puffin Sound, waters I knew well and felt confident on. Then half way across Red Wharf Bay the wind died. We wallowed about for a while, sails flapping and checking the time, I decided that Amlwch was out of the question. The motor went on, the sails went down and we headed for Moelfre. I checked the Pilot and noted that Moelfre Bay was a safe anchorage in anything but easterlies and what wind there had been that day was south westerly. Perfect.

I threw the hook down about fifty yards from the stony beach and settled down with a noggin for an hour to assure myself that the anchor was holding. The tide was falling and she stayed just where I'd put her. The weather forecast gave 'South to South Westerly 2 to 3 for the next 24 hours, perhaps locally South East 4 to 5, gusting 6' — I was safe. The 'locally' couldn't mean Moelfre, could it? Not in the whole of the Irish Sea.

A gentle row ashore in the dinghy found me beached at the foot of a flight of steps leading up to The Moelfre Arms. Even more perfect. And then I met the gentleladies, well, not so much met as pushed myself into their conversation. The feeling of proud ownership of my own yacht had overcome me and I simply had to show off. Like a drowning man needs a rope, I need admiration. I've always been like that, ask Mother. And here it was in bucketfulls.

They were positively gushing in their praise of Rip-Rap's beautiful lines, her size, (I'd told them she was 33 feet long, not 23 and, as there were no other boats near her there was nothing to compare her with) and how I managed to sail her single-handed. This evening could get no better.

"It must be simply thrilling," said the lackey. "Don't cha know."

"Yes. It's a great challenge, but you ladies must be used to great challenges, I can tell."

"Yes." It was the leader. "We've been toyin' with the idea of a craft of some kind for quite a while, haven't we Eddie?"

" Er, yes Vonnie, yes."

Horsefeathers, I thought. But I didn't say it.

"Super," was what I actually said. "Perhaps you'd like to come over, have a look and a nightcap maybe? There's some whisky on board."

"No," the leader again, "we really must be orf, thanks all the same. Piddle — before we depart, ducks?"

I'd hoped she was talking to the lackey, her squint made it difficult to read.

"No, ta, dearest. I'm fine."

"Right. Orf we go then. Well, it's been really lovely meeting you and we both wish you all the very best of luck with your lovely, lovely boat, don't we Eds?"

"Yes, indeed we do. All the very best. Cheerio, Pete."

"Cheerio."

"Cheerio."

And with that they swept out.

I breathed a huge sigh of relief — what if they had come aboard? I would have felt just a tad embarrassed at lying about her size, but I was pretty safe in reality. They had their sensible shoes on.

"You're dragging. Look."

I looked in the direction of the Coxwain's outstretched arm and I didn't have to look very far. About fifteen feet, actually, to the cliffs at the westerly end of Moelfre Bay.

I'd done about a hundred yards or so from where I'd dropped anchor the previous night, without even knowing. That 'South East 4 to 5, gusting 6 locally' had meant Moelfre. Why didn't they tell me? And anyway, they'd got that wrong. It felt more like 6 to 7, gusting 8!

"Pull your anchor up and get the hell out of here. It's going to get worse."

I shot up the foredeck and started to tug on the chain. She wouldn't budge. I wrapped both hands around what slack I could get hold of and just as I tugged the mightiest tug, a big one hit the bows. Rip-Rap bucked, both hands were flattened against the deck and blood started pumping.

"Can't budge it," I screamed across to the Lifeboat.

"Tie a fender to it, drop the lot and come back later. Just get the hell out of here."

Good idea that, tying the fender on. I'd never have thought of it myself, not in the state I was in right then anyway. I did as he said, starting the motor and giving myself some way on, then, dropping the fender over the side, I gunned the motor and got the hell out of there, as instructed.

I was half way across Red Wharf Bay heading straight into this fearsome wind before I really came to my senses. The bleeding had eased a bit, but blood was everywhere. The cockpit and starboard side-deck looked just like the namestyle on the side of the hull, only this lot didn't spell anything comprehensible. Looked more like an infant school-sized catering can of alphabet soup that had done a short burst in a blender.

We made it back to the mooring around lunchtime, me and Rip-Rap. Bloodied, yet unbowed.

The wind had abated in the Straits and it was all quite calm by the time I stepped through the front door of The Mostyn and fell into Rita's arms. Rita is the very lovely landlady, she cares for me for some reason. Anyway, she had me bandaged up and on my way back to Moelfre in no time. I had to arrange to get my anchor back.

I stuck a tenner in the Lifeboat box and rang the local Secretary of the RNLI. He suggested I talk to the Moelfre lobster man Gwyn, who had a little boat and might help me out. I contacted him through the pub landlord and he said he'd have it for me next weekend. I went home.

It has a postscript, this yarn. I went back to Moelfre the next weekend, as arranged and picked up the seriously valuable ground tackle. I gave Gwyn a twenty pound note (he'd had to get a diver to it) and he told me I could've stayed there all summer if I'd wanted.

The anchor was stuck round a sewage outfall pipe!

Chapter 4

THE WEST ANGLESEY NAUTICAL CRUISING ASSOCIATION

In which I tell more tales of yotting adventures, introduce you to my girlfriend Beth, daughter and son-in-law and other close friends, as well as my attempt to get an RYA International Certificate of Competence.

" I feel very comfortable with you, Beth."
"And I feel comfortable with you too, Peter Marsh."

I was gazing into the clearest, most beautiful eyes it's ever been my privilege to gaze into, since Brigitte Bardot's that is. Brigitte was seducing me, her eyes so beautifully set, wide and cat-like above that pouting smile, the tousled blonde head attached to that magnificent body lying on a beach at St Tropez, and I was lying on my school dormitory bed a million or more miles away.

I allowed myself to glance down momentarily and take in the wide easy smile, the smile I'd first seen a couple of weeks earlier in Knutsford Wine Bar. It was all my mother's fault.

Beth is a friend of Mother's, despite over thirty years' age difference. She's an extremely talented writer of children's books and had had some dispute over copyright with an American publisher. Mother had phoned to ask if I could help in some way and I'd put Beth on to one of my erstwhile early doors buddies, a solicitor who specialises in copyright law. He'd sorted out Beth's problem for her and she'd rung to thank me.

That had been months ago, almost a year and I'd forgotten all about her. Then Mother telephoned and suggested I rang Beth and arrange a meeting. I must say that her voice sounded good on the phone, but I couldn't imagine what she looked like. I did ring and we fixed a day to meet in the Wine Bar. I asked Mother how I would know her and she replied, 'You'll know Beth, it's those eyes.' That's all, 'it's those eyes.' It was those eyes.

As I walked into the Wine Bar, no, as I looked through the window as I walked towards the Wine Bar, I saw those eyes. They are a haunting greeny-blue colour and they haunt me now as I write these words over a thousand miles away from them. I have photos, of course, but no photograph can do them or the smile justice. I squeezed her hand under the table and I felt like the luckiest man on earth. Fifty three years old and fixed up by my mum!

I had to look away, Gaz had just started to make his speech.

It was the Christmas Luncheon of the West Anglesey Nautical Cruising Association and, as our leader, it was Gazzer's turn to make the speech.

All those months ago, barbecueing on Pilot's Cove beach, Big Dave had suggested we form a joke club and it had happened. We'd had the inaugural do in October, at the Alvanley Arms, Cotebrook and all the yotties mentioned thus far were there and one or two others, but not Duncan, of course. He was on a sailing weekend in the Lake District with his brother.

I'd made the inaugural speech, naming the club (WANCA for short) and appointing the Flag Officers. Every yacht club has Flag Officers and the WANCAs were to be no exception. I did feel however that Commodore was a stuffy title and decided that the WANCAs would have a Big Knob instead, and because he'd introduced most of us to off-shore yottin', who better than Gaz to be the first Big Knob. Big Dave was his Rear and I was the Vice. We appointed Dunc as Social Secretary (in loco absentis) and Tim, Racing Secretary. Big Dave's missus was Chairperson of the Ladies Committee, her culinary efforts at the Bar-B-Q were unsurpassed, despite a strong bid from Gaz, who was out to impress his boss.

Young Paul, who'd been with Gaz, Luke and I on that sailing weekend some five years previously, was there with his fiancé Jane, both of them instructors at the National Watersports Centre at Plas Menai. We see quite a lot of them, whizzing about in safety boats and shouting at people doing funny things in dinghies, so it seemed singularly appropriate that we make them Safety Officers. That was the committee and here we were at the Xmasfest, same venue, but more people. We'd sent ripples through the dinghy sailing club and had to close the doors at 26 for this do. Even Duncan and his good lady were there. Everybody wanted to join, all that is except the stuffed ones. The WANCAs are destined to be exclusive — you have to be invited and the Committee has to unanimously approve the invitees.

Gaz sat down to much applause and mirth, then old Padded Shoulders stood up.

Padded Shoulders is Duncan's lady, mother of his youngest and so named because of her somewhat bizarre dress sense when yottin'. Dunc's told her that Menai Bridge is Monte Carlo and I swear she believes him. She takes it in good part though and for this event had put in double the amount of padding. The WANCAs do make every effort to extract the urine from each other.

Louise, for that is the name she goes by, is also in possession of a part-time stutter, I say part-time because Duncan has told us that she doesn't stutter when arguing with him, which is a damned nuisance because it doesn't give him much time to think. So it came as something of a surprise to all when she stood up and declared that she would reply on behalf of the ladies.

It was a splendid speech, entirely stutter-free and I repeat it here in its entirety.

"Thank you, on behalf of the ladies and I'm so pleased that you have at last found a suitable collective noun for yourselves."

She sat down to a cheer that could've been heard in Chester.

We sat there all afternoon — nobody wanted to go and Mike the landlord didn't complain, there were pound signs in his eyes. Much discussion took place about the date and venue for the next do and it was decided that we should have a launching weekend in March. Having half-organised this Xmasfest, and turned up for it, Duncan declared that he would take full responsibility for the next event.

Everybody held their breath, but not for long — the Boat Show intervened.

"Will we be able to go out and meet Lara, Dad?"
"Don't see why not," I replied.

Luke and I were the only WANCAs on the coach, typically. The Boat Show is a must when you're actually a boat owner. There's a tremendous temptation to buy all sorts of useless gadgets to screw to your vessel in order to make it go faster, handle or look better and when you do you spend hours wondering why the hell you bothered. That's yottin'.

I don't think I've mentioned my eldest yet, so I'll tell you a little in order for you to appreciate the next bit.

Lara is my stepdaughter, in fact — she was four when I met her mother, but her natural father died and I adopted her as my own when the ex-Mrs Marsh was pregnant with Luke. After the adoption hearing Lara looked up at me and asked if she could call me Daddy now. At that moment there were tears in my eyes and she's caused a few since. We shall not dwell on bad times — this is supposed to be an entertaining tale.

When she was eighteen and in her A-level year, Lara made the decision to take a year out between school and university, a 'gap' year I believe they call it. I was heartily in favour, her mother, the educationalist, wasn't.

Talking to Nick, a pub manager of my acquaintance one evening, my attention was drawn to a cricket bat propped up behind the bar. It had been signed by the entire England and Pakistan teams and a sign on the bat said, 'Raffle — for the Project Trust'. I asked Nick what the Project Trust was and he outlined its objectives — it was an organisation which sent gap year kids away to far flung places. His son was doing it and had to raise a tidy sum to pay for his year; hence the raffle for the bat, just one of many fund-raising ideas young Ian had had. I dashed home and told Lara of all this and she sounded very enthusiastic, so much so that she asked me to fix up a meeting with young Ian. He sold her on the idea and she applied.

To cut a long story short, Lara was selected and sent to Cuba for a year, teaching English at Havana University to students who had previously been taught Russian. These were the days when Castro realised that he was going to have to do something to shake off his heavily subsidised past and move closer to reality. Lara had a great year — she went so full of admiration for Castro and his beliefs and came back loathing him. And she'd met Cristian, a pony-tailed, earring-festooned young Cuban, one of her students and destined to become her husband, and a more delightful young man you'd be hard pressed to meet. At the time of the Boat Show they were living in London, Lara studying hard for her finals at UCL, Cris having got a first at Havana and now working at the highly exalted job of shop assistant in a Thorntons Chocolate Cabin, much the kind of career you'd expect for a young man with a first class honours degree in English.

Luke and I had done two hours at the Show, we'd phoned Lara and made a rendezvous and I'd bought a Solar Battery Charger, essential tackle for living aboard Rip-Rap in the S of F. Then we made for the exit and our pre-arranged meeting with Lara and Cris.

After a couple of drinks Lara went to the toilet and Cris leant over to whisper in my ear. He'd booked EasyJet to Nice as a surprise for Lara when she finished her exams and wanted to borrow my 'Rough Guide'. He's got a curiously frugal mind, Cris, quite happy to spend a couple of hundred on flights but not ten on a 'Rough Guide'. Still, you have to admire his thinking, he'd heard me slagging it off when they came to visit at Christmas, obviously realised that I would have no further use for it and a polite request would make it his. It did.

I said I'd send it to him but he said 'no', he was coming to Cheshire in February for my mother's birthday and he'd pick it up then.

I gave the kids a tenner to go and get a pizza and went back to the Show, telling Luke I'd see him on the coach.

The Guinness stand, every hour, on the hour. It's always been thus and it's amazing who you meet. This year was Tony and Tina's turn.

41

They used to be next door neighbours years ago and I'd introduced Tony to yottin'. At one time we'd shared a 505 and raced it together, but Tony lost interest and went off to buy a Jaguar 22 and do his off-shore bit. He now owned a lovely old wooden Folkboat and is a fully fledged WANCA. They'd sat opposite Beth and me at the Xmasfest and said they would be going to the Boat Show, but they'd missed the coach and decided to drive instead. We had a pleasant hour sipping the Liffey water and talking about my up-coming venture. I got the feeling that Tina was seriously jealous — it's just the sort of thing she'd like to do, if there weren't kids in the way, so to rub salt into the wound I showed them my Solar Battery Charger.

"That'll be no bloody use to you," said Tony. "You'll need a proper trickle charger to keep up with the amount of lekkie you'll be using."

He'd got me worried and I'd only had the thing a few hours.

Tony is an aircraft engineer at Manchester Airport and he knows about these sorts of things. He's even got aircraft batteries on his Folkboat. He was to be proved partially right, but you'll have to wait for that bit. What you don't have to wait too much longer for is the story of the WANCAs 1997 summer holiday, taken partially alone and partially together. Although the Association hadn't yet been officially formed, it'll give you an idea of what it's like to be a WANCA.

"Rip-Rap, Rip-Rap, Rip-Rap, this is Rufus, Rufus. Come in please."

There was a hint of anxiety in the voice and he'd missed off one 'Rufus'. It must be urgent, but he must know that I'm upstairs, clinging onto the tiller for my life and the radio's downstairs, in the relative comfort and warmth of the cabin, lucky thing. Duncan was only half a mile in front of me, heading straight for Barmouth fairway buoy and actually not that far from it. The wind had got up, the sea was choppy and the sky was an ominous grey.

"Rip-Rap, Rip-Rap. This is Rufus. Come in... please!"

I peered over the coachroof and saw Rufus cavorting about all over the place. Duncan was obviously downstairs on the radio and had abandoned the tiller. I did the same.

The previous day three boats, Rip-Rap and I, Rufus and Duncan, and Tony on his Folkboat called 'Fenella', with a friend whose name escapes me but is known by Tony's kids and therefore subsequently us, as Penfold, had left the relative safety of the Straits and headed for Barmouth.

It'd been partly Tony's idea, Tina had booked a holiday apartment there for her and the kids and Tony's idea was to join them and get in a bit of family holiday yottin'. Dunc and I had an idea that we might go some place that week, so we joined Tony.

We'd sailed out of the Straits and headed for Porth Dinlleyn as an overnight stop. In the process of throwing down the anchors Tony had got a rope caught round his prop and had to go into the water to free it. It was freezing cold and Tony very nearly gave up. It was only Penfold holding him underwater that got the offensive bit of string off. I've always thought of Tony as Danger Mouse ever since but I wouldn't call him that to his face. He'd knock me block off — or Tina would.

Ty Coch was closed — always is on a Monday, says a sign on the door, so we motored in the dinghies over to another establishment which purveyed the tawny foaming stuff in Morfa Nefyn. Thank God I'd had the sense to leave Rip-Rap's masthead light on or we'd never have found our way back to the boats.

The next day's sail, through Bardsey Sound and across Hell's Mouth was breathtaking. Conditions could not have been better. A lot of blue stuff up above, with a few white fluffy things and a steady 20 knots of wind from the south west. Perfect reaching conditions. The three boats were in close company until we got to St Tudwal's Islands and Dunc decided to make a break for it. It's the racing background, he simply can't sit back and enjoy himself. He's got to be the first there.

Tony had other ideas, the Folkboat was faster and Tony knew it. Off he went and very quickly overhauled Rufus, drawing a good mile out before he approached the Barmouth fairway.

And that was the situation when I heard Duncan's call.

"Rufus, Rufus. This is Rip-Rap. Channel six nine. Over."

43

We always listen on Channel 16, it's the emergency channel and the one everybody listens to, but the Coastguards get a bit miffed if you start having a natter on said channel. So me and Dunc always switch to 69 — it appeals.

"Look old bean, we're in a spot of trouble here. It's wind against a falling tide and I'm none too happy about what state the Bar's going to be in when we get there. Over."

"Neither am I. Could be empty, could be full of rampant tottie, who knows. Over."

I was looking forward to re-acquainting myself with Barmouth Yacht Club, this time as an official, 100% genuine, visiting yottie.

Dunc's voice was very angry when he made his reply. Livid, in fact.

"Can't you think of anything other than beer and women, you mindless moron? I mean Barmouth Bar, that fucking great sandbank we've got to cross! Over."

Oo-err. That'd got his hackles up, the tetchy little terrier.

By this time Rip-Rap had got her hackles up as well and was gyrating about like a circus woman on horseback. It was time to cut the banter and make serious decisions.

"OK. What do you suggest? Over."

"We turn round and head back to Pwllheli, right. It'll be OK there in the Marina. Over."

"Follow me. Over and out."

Turning round and heading back I had half a mile on him, but he still beat me. One day I'll get my own back.

We had a great time in Pwllheli Yacht Club and I bumped into some old yottin' mates who I hadn't seen for some time. A good evening all round, but nothing compared with what was to come!

"Pete, this is Jane," Tina politely informed me.

The Barmouth YC bar was moderately full and there was assorted tottie, rampant and otherwise. I was being introduced to one right now, but at the time I wasn't sure which of the above categories Jane fell into. I was hoping it would be the former, she's quite a looker and turned out to be the ex of an old sparring partner of mine, the owner of the holiday apartment which Tina had rented here in Barmouth.

It's worth mentioning Richard at this point because he will enter the tale at least once more.

I've mentioned that Tony and Tina were once neighbours of mine — so was Richard, same house but on the other side. In fact, it's my fault we got Richard as a neighbour in the first place. He came to visit one day, liked our house so much he bought the one next door.

I'd first met Richard at the dinghy sailing club, he also raced a 505 with the apposite name of 'Bummer's Rush'. I took to him instantly, the name of his boat emblazoned in foot-high red letters on the yellow hull caused the stuffed ones to go positively apoplectic. Then, at the midsummer Commodore's Weekend Bar-B-Q, with entertainment provided by a really bad jazz band, Richard further upset the establishment by pulling out his guitar and giving an impromptu alternative concert at the end of one of the jetties. It was so much better than the paid-for entertainment that quite a crowd gathered round and thunderous applause was given.

I invited Richard to crew for me at that year's Dinghy Week.

He accepted, we took his guitar and my banjo and did the impromptu thing all over the Lleyn Peninsula. It was a great week, Richard was smashing with the kids who were only nine and three at the time and we all got on really well. He was also an extremely competent crew, fearless to the point of insanity, just what you need on a 505. He also provided me with great entertainment when offering ripostes to the other sailor's shouts for 'Water'. I've never been too hot on racing rules, I know a few basics and I've got by.

Neither, it transpired was Richard, but if in doubt, bamboozle them, was his philosophy.

"Spoon yer bows.", "Straighten yer baggywrinkles." and "Abaft yer thwart." would come the reply to the constant requests for 'water at the mark', or wherever.

We sailed through the fleet happy in the knowledge that they thought we knew more than they did. That year I got my best results ever and some kudos in the bar afterwards when the guitar and banjo came out.

Now you'd think that Richard would make ideal WANCA material and indeed in those days, he would have. If only he'd stayed like that, but sadly Richard has turned into what can only be described as boorish. He bought an off-shore yacht, a cottage in Nefyn and got himself elected onto the committee of Nefyn Yacht Club. His attempts to change the style of the club got him booted out and he moved his attentions to Barmouth YC where he tried to do exactly the same thing. Worse than that, he bought the house next door to the club and proceeded to fence off part of their land as his. You can imagine that he's none too popular with the committee and, for that matter, most of the members. Yet he's so arrogant and thick-skinned he still frequents the place and imposes himself on folk.

And one such of those folk was Jane, who having initially been taken in by Richard's charisma, which to the uninformed he undoubtably has, was severely hurt by him and was, at the time I was introduced to her, still smarting.

Jane is a divorcee, some ten years older than Richard and therefore within my potential age bracket, and as previously mentioned, quite a stunner. So our holiday in and around Barmouth was already taking a rapidly upturning swing. Dunc and I had only arrived from Pwllheli ten minutes before.

After a few ales and jocular banter we paid the Harbourmaster a visit in order to pay our dues.

"You'll be staying most of the week then, storm-bound," he said.

That wasn't our plan at the time. We rather thought of an overnight here and then off to Aberdovey and other points south, perhaps returning later in the week on our way back. Then the kind man informed us that we'd never get out across the Bar, probably for three or four days. He'd got a weatherfax and showed it to us. It looked grim; South Westerlies, Force 6 and above, for the foreseeable future. Dunc was crestfallen, I wasn't all that bothered. The thought of being storm-bound in Jane's arms for a few days and nights was mighty appealing.

Sadly, dear reader, it was not to be. So badly had Richard hurt the delightful lady that she ran a mile when a potential pal loomed up, another reason for me to dislike the man.

The three days in Barmouth were, however, most enjoyable. Dunc decided to go home and score some brownie points with Padded Shoulders and I stayed, sleeping alone on the boat, drinking liberally in BYC, even walking over to Rydd-y-Benllech for old times' sake.

I bought some bits in the chandlery and spent some time screwing them onto Rip-Rap.

One of Gazzer's gadgets on Hunca Munca is a thing called a Tillattenda, a bit of rope and a clamp which holds the tiller still and keeps you pointing in roughly the direction you want to travel, whilst you go downstairs to put the kettle on, use the radio or splash your boots. I've always liked this device, so handy for single-handed yottin', but never seen one in any chandlery I've been in, the one in Barmouth being no exception. Some time was spent in discussion with the Chandler, who had heard of Tillattendas, but never had one in stock, and we worked out a judicious way of bodging one up with some bits and pieces he did have.

It was this device I was attempting to fit when I heard a very husky female call from the quay. It was Jane, looking stunning in tight white jeans and T-shirt.

I dropped what I was doing, leapt into the dinghy and motored over. She wanted to have a look at Rip-Rap as she'd told me that it was only a matter of time before she bought a yacht of her own. I have no compunction in showing people my pride and joy, not even damned attractive ones and this was going to be an opportunity for me to re-kindle my seduction of same.

Jane loved everything about Rip-Rap and when I pulled out the Hostess I thought she was going to have an orgasm. Women do like that sort of thing on a boat, but generally speaking, women don't like yottin'. The few that do have usually got great big bums, no tits and hideous faces, but I'd found the exception.

I asked Jane to shift her prettily formed and perfectly proportioned bum to one side, in order that I might get to the wine cellar, and pulled the cork out of a chilled bottle of Muscadet. Two glasses were filled and we clinked a toast to her imaginary future vessel. Then Tony arrived in his dinghy and invited Jane to see his Folkboat. Insensitive sod, couldn't he see I was in the process of trying to get her jeans off? Some pal!

She went with him and I followed with the wine. Then she fell in love with Fenella.

I've got to admit, she's a lovely old boat, all natural varnished wood and polished brass, the kind of boat that turns a girl's head. I'd lost. However, Tony did have his family and very daunting wife less than fifty yards away in the holiday flatlet, and I was on my own. It would only be a minor setback.

The wine bottle quickly emptied itself and I suggested we repair to the YC, it being a few minutes past opening time. I stepped into my dinghy and Jane joined me (I don't think she wanted to give Tina the wrong idea, should she see us all going ashore) and Tony stepped into his dinghy. Well, not actually into, onto.

His foot located the gunwale and he put all his weight onto it. The dinghy capsized and Tony went in.

This was the third time he'd taken a swim on this trip. The Porth Dinlleyn rope incident, the day before, when he and Penfold had run aground in the Straits and he'd had to get out and push, and now this. I couldn't suppress my mirth and I was still giggling at the sight of his face as it surfaced and spurted out a plume of water, when Tina and the kids arrived in the YC bar half an hour later.

The story was going to be told, so she might as well hear it from Tony. I went to the bar to fetch ale and returned to hear Tina's response to Tony's tale.

"Wanker!"

She didn't know then how absolutely correct she was going to be. Almost psychic. This was two weeks after the Pilot's Cove Bar-B-Q and my mind was already working on that idea.

It could have been that comment which started the whole thing off. We'll never know.

Dunc returned on the Friday night with Tim, who'd left Black Dog at Abersoch after the Regatta a fortnight before. He would sail with Dunc, we'd stop at Abersoch, pick up Black Dog and continue round to the Straits. Four boats in company — great! There was much discussion about the weather of the past few days and we wondered how our other friends had fared. Gaz had taken Hunca Munca down to South Wales on his own and Big Dave had taken a motley crew across to Ireland. Gazzer's tale would unfold upon his return to Port Dinorwic the next Sunday — Dave has drawn a veil over his trip and I doubt if we'll ever know what really happened. 'Disaster' is the only word I've ever managed to get out of him, and I can imagine when hearing Gazzer's yarn that some similar things might have happened to Dave and his crew on Trenarth.

"So there I was standing in Newquay Yacht Club bar, dressed up to the nines in grey slacks, blazer and yottie tie, with beer in hand, talking to one of the locals. 'Which yacht is yours then?' he asked me and I looked out of the window to point her out to him. Just in time, as it happens. She'd picked up her mooring and was just sliding out of the harbour. 'That one,' I said, dropping my beer and legging it. I bumped into a` yuppie coming into the clubhouse, grabbed his mobile phone and rang the Coastguard. Then legged it down to the quayside, waved a tenner at a fisherman and we set off in his smack. We found Hunca Munca two miles away, doing about three knots despite having a ton or so of ground tackle hanging off her bow."

He does have some adventures, our Gaz. And that was the tamest thing that had happened to him on his week's holiday.

When the wind really started to get up on the Tuesday, the day Dunc and I discovered we were storm-bound in Barmouth, he found a sheltered cove and threw the hook down. The wind was coming straight off the shore and the tide was falling. OK, you'd think, sensible thing to do. But what he didn't realise was that this particular cove had a gently sloping shore and as the tide dropped Gaz found himself in very shallow water, right in the breakers and no chance of re-locating. He wound up the drop keel and rode out the night in hurricane force winds, Hunca Munca being thrown this way and that. There was no way Gaz could sleep, he just had to hang on. The book he'd been reading when the wind had really started to get up had disappeared the next day and he was miffed, he'd just got to a good bit. He found the book eventually, some weeks later. It had gone down the centreboard casing and jammed the keel.

So bad was the wind, the sea state as well, that the rest of Gazzer's week was spent quite a way out in the Irish Sea, well away from potential trouble but, by Saturday night he was very, very tired and coming through Bardsey Sound. He poked Hunca Munca's nose out of the Sound, pointed her in the general direction of South Stack, fixed the Tillatenda and went downstairs to sleep. The thinking here was that the sound of the breakers on South Stack rocks would wake him should the alarm not work. It doesn't always. Fortunately he awoke before getting there and turned for the haven of peace we call the Menai Straits.

I watched as Hunca Munca motored slowly towards me. I got into my dinghy and went over as Gaz picked up his mooring. He was so tired he literally couldn't speak and he looked awful; drawn, grey face, deep-set eyes that just stared blankly. I left him to sleep and motored back to Rip-Rap. This was going to be some yarn, I could tell, and I couldn't contain my excitement.

It was that night in the Garddfon Arms that all this came out, as we sank the odd pint and yarned. God, I love Gaz, I'm glad he's still with us.

The WANCAs launching weekend do loomed and I booked rooms at the Liverpool Arms, Menai Bridge, the venue Duncan had chosen for said do. The rooms are not at the Liddy actually, rather at the Auckland, another pub just around the corner and owned by the same people, the formidable Mr and Mrs Thickett.

I'd once had a run-in with Mrs Thickett, at the pre-race breakfast before the Round Anglesey. I'd asked for another cup of tea and was told that my ticket was for one cup, 'One. Right!' I didn't argue: you don't argue with Mrs Thickett.

Now, here she was on the other end of the phone and said she recognised my voice. If she'd put two and two together I'd be doomed, but I suppose, as I was just in the process of handing her several portraits of the Queen in a russet hue, she'd perhaps let bygones be bygones.

"Two rooms, for two people? It'll be 25 quid each, that's the best I can do. £35, if you're prepared to share."

My relationship with Beth had blossomed, but the one thing she cannot stand about me is my snoring, not a lot of people can. The various yotties who've slept on the same vessel have either had to put up with it or gone elsewhere, if they were able.

A gang of us once took Hunca Munca up to Tarbert on Loch Fyne for Rover Week, a huge Regatta attended by anything up to 400 yachts. The sight of that many boats in Tarbert harbour is one to behold. They raft you up, twenty boats together and we were on raft F. One night, in one of the four or five pubs in Tarbert, whose landlords double the price of drinks for the week, I overheard a fellow say,

"Have you heard that bloke snoring? I think it's on raft F."

I turned to him and said,

"Yes, what raft are you on?".

"B", he said.

I didn't reply, but Tim slept in his car that week, half a mile away.

I asked Mrs Thickett how far apart the rooms would be and she assured me that she could put us at either ends of the pub, if we wished. We wished, but I think Beth would've preferred to be in Beaumaris.

It was a splendid night, much in the mould of what WANCA do's were being moulded in.

"I just love the way you get people together and then sit back and watch what happens," Beth once said to me.

She's right really. I do love people-watching, but if I've chosen the people who should be watched, then so much the better.

I'd had a couple of parties over the Christmas and New Year season at my wonderfully renovated cottage and, of course, Beth had been there.

At the first party, my heart had sunk when I saw a photographer friend and his wife arrive. This was not because I don't like them, they wouldn't have been invited if I didn't like them, it was simply that I suddenly realised that they were not going to fit in. They didn't know anybody and there was nobody there that they could talk to. Big mistake.

For the next party, Beth suggested that I might invite some of my advertising friends, then Dave and Suzanne (said photographer and wife) would feel more at home. I did, and it happened, very successfully.

Now, here we were at the Liddy Arms and right next to us, new recruits to the WANCAs, Neil and his amazing Norwegian wife Randi, a name that conjures up all kind of things and sends my Spellchecker into gyrations. In fairness to Neil, he would've been one of the founder members, but business and other travels had kept him away from the Straits during the year the WANCAs really got together. This year, during my sojourn in the S of F, I sincerely hoped that Neil would take my place as Vice Big Knob (in loco parentis, whatever the hell that means).

Neil is a seriously good yottie and another keen and highly successful racer.

The WANCAs attended the dinghy club's Boxing Day Regatta, purely to indulge in the social side of things, all of us that is, except Neil and Dunc. They raced, and came first and second respectively.

During his year away from the Straits Neil had bought two boats, an Elizabethan 23 and an Evolution 19, Hunca Munca's little sister. He'd taken the Evolution to Norway where Randi has a house on an island in Oslo Fjord. They are appealing little boats, Jane and I had looked at one in the boatyard at Barmouth and I'd said it would suit her ideally, but she couldn't afford it. As part of my seduction strategy I did consider offering to help her out, but I've never paid for it yet and besides Beth came along. Glad I didn't now.

Neil told me of the life they have when spending time at Randi's house.

You get a phone call, sometimes in the middle of the night, because it doesn't really go dark during the summer. Then you jump into your boat, sail over to someone else's island and party. Sounds great, I was really quite jealous.

He told me that he was bringing the Elizabethan called 'Aquarius' to the Straits for the summer after his father had spent some time doing a renovation job on her. I looked forward to seeing her and he said he was sure there would be a time when we could sail together as Rip-Rap was on her trailer in Macclesfield Canal Marina awaiting her departure for France, which I planned for mid-May.

I'd taken her to Macc the previous October, partly to see what she was like to tow behind the ageing Volvo and partly so that she would be near to home in order for me to screw bits on and generally prepare her for the trip. I'd had to bear the brunt of some remarks from my drinking buddies who'd given me some stick about having a boat in a pub car park in Bangor last year. All winter I got similar stick about having said boat in the car park of Hovis Mill. Technically, neither of those locations were strictly accurate, adjacent, not actually in. But then GPS's aren't always that accurate.

Sailing down the Straits with Dunc on our way to the first WANCA Bar-B-Q of the year, his GPS had us somewhere up Caernarfon High Street.

The Bar-B-Q was planned at the launching weekend do, a weekend during which not one boat was launched. We'd done a lot of talking about it but no doing it.

Now here we were, late April and a fine Spring day, Neil was supposed to be with us, but wasn't, so Beth and I had hitched a ride with Dunc and family on Rufus, whilst Luke went with Tim, nearly all the WANCAs on our way to Abermenai (it was supposed to be Pilot's Cove but inevitably the plans got changed).

This was Beth's introduction to yottin' and a better baptism you couldn't imagine.

As explained, she's neurotic about where she's going to sleep, and no amount of sun, a light breeze filling the colourful spinnaker, a glass of chilled Chardonnay and good company could quell her fears that she might end up shoe-horned into a damp berth on the same boat as the man who can snore for England. She admitted as much to me that night in Duncan's cottage. He wanted to spend the night with his family aboard

Rufus, the first night his little five year old Victoria would spend afloat, so he'd lent us the cottage. God bless him, he'd probably saved my relationship with Beth — she'd threatened to get in my car and drive herself home if I didn't find her a B&B or something suitable.

The Bar-B-Q was tremendous, Big Dave and Pauline had Gaz with them on Trenarth, Tim, his current lady, another Jane, her son Matthew and Luke on Black Dog, and us lot on Rufus.

The first sausages had been consumed when a cheer went up as the blue-hulled Aquarius hove into view with Neil and his daughter Jenny aboard. We'd seen Tony and Tina, they'd taken Fenella round to Pwllheli where Tony had booked a berth for the summer. He was fed up of losing days sailing because of the nature of his job and missing the tide all the time. From Pwllheli he could go out at any state of the tide and that would suit him better. They couldn't make the Bar-B-Q though, he'd got to go to work. So it was nearly a full complement of WANCAs who partied the afternoon away at Abermenai.

The next day Beth, Luke and I drove back to Port Dinorwic for the 12 o'clock rendezvous Dunc had set for the return trip through the Swellies to Menai Bridge and his mooring. As we drove past the Swellies I saw the unmistakable fleet of Trenarth, Black Dog, Rufus and Aquarius motoring through. Dunc, as usual, had got the tide times wrong. We turned around and went back to Menai pier where we saw them gaily sailing past.

"I know where they're going. Come on you two."

We jumped into the Volvo and drove down the Straits to The Gazelle, a favourite yottie watering hole right on the shoreline opposite Bangor Pier. Sure enough, they all picked up moorings and came ashore. Copious ales were consumed and we got a ride back to Menai on Aquarius, Luke once more going with Tim to look after young Matthew. He's great with kids is Luke, always has been ever since he was one himself.

It was another pleasant afternoon and Beth had her first yottie pee, her feet sticking out from under the modesty curtain Neil's dad had fitted. She also found a Solar Battery Charger down there and brandished it proudly.

"Hey Pete, you've got one of these things on Rip-Rap."
I have, I bought it at the Boat Show, although I'd never used it.
So I asked Neil if they were any good and he replied,
"Not a clue. Never used it. It's one of those things that father
said I had to have. That's what happens with a father like mine,
he tells me what I should have and I pay for it."

Early May, and it didn't look as if I was going to get away on
schedule. More stick from drinking buddies, 'Oh you'll never get
there,' or 'You might make a fortnight's holiday in September',
that kind of thing. There was however a genuine reason for the
delay, the obtaining by fair means or foul of my ICC, or
International Certificate of Competence.

My early days of off-shore yottin' had mostly been done with
one James Clarke Snr and/or his son, also called James. They are
known as Jim and Jimmy respectively, to avoid confusion, and
they are both fully qualified RYA Instructors. So, as I'd learnt most
of what I know from them, I've never seen any need for making
what qualifications I may have to yott formal. But at the launching
weekend I'd had a chat with young Paul, now a Yachtmaster
Instructor himself, and he'd mentioned, at first almost casually,
that I would have to have an ICC if I wanted to sail in France. We
discussed various ways in which I might be able to obtain this
vital piece of paperwork and he said, in truth, the only way was
to go to Plas Menai and do a weekend course. I'd booked it, but
the first weekend I could get was early in June.

Whilst waiting for June to arrive I bumped into Big Jim and
asked him if he could wangle an ICC for me. He said 'no', he'd
retired now and young Jimmy was working in Northern Ireland.
Then he suggested Peter Boon and said, 'Buy Pete a drink and
he'll sign one off for you.'

Now this sounded hopeful, but I had my doubts. Peter had been
the OD for that Puffin Island Race we'd been penalised on all
those years ago and he played everything strictly by the book. I
doubted that he would deem a free pint quite sufficient for
bending the RYA's rules. I was right, the answer was 'no', but he
suggested I ring one David Leinster, a Yachtmaster Instructor who

had a yacht somewhere on the Straits. He might agree to take me out on that and give me my practical. I rang Gaz to see if he knew this Leinster — he did.

"Christ," he said, "Don't go to him. He takes no prisoners. Forget it and go to Plas Menai. It's your best bet."

So I sent off a cheque for £136 and awaited the day.

Then the letter from the Chambre Syndicale Regional des Industries Nautiques (CSRIN) arrived, with a sheaf of photocopied A4 French gobble-dee-gook not a word of which I understood, but gathered it was the laws under which I would have to sail. More of that later.

"Excuse me," I said to the rotund and florid man with the benign face, "Are you my Skipper?"

I'd attended the course induction at Plas Menai, during which I could not gather any useful piece of information whatsoever, apart from the boats we'd be spending the weekend on were at Port Dinorwic Marina, a fact I already knew as I'd seen them there many times. I'd driven to Port Dinorwic, parked my car and walked to the Marina. That was where the florid-faced one was with other faces I vaguely recognised from the induction. They were just sort of milling about.

"Probably," he replied and picked up a clip-board with papers clipped to it. "Let's see. I've got Terry and Sue here," he indicated a middle-aged, rather plump couple, "Jason and Victoria," a fit-looking yuppie couple, "so, if you're Peter Marsh, then yes."

I looked gloomily at my companions for the weekend and my heart sank.

As previously mentioned I do like to pick the company I spend time with but I knew there was nothing much I could do about it, so I loaded my kit aboard the Westerly Fulmar 'Menai II', and we sat down for the Skipper's briefing. I was going to have to do this myself at some stage over the weekend so I listened intently, as we all sat round the table which was just marginally smaller than Rip-Rap's cabin. After he'd gone through his briefing he asked us all in turn what we wanted to gain from this weekend, the others went first.

Terry and Sue were here for the third time and hoping to get their Competent Crew tickets. Jason and Victoria already had theirs, had bought a 21' trailer-sailer and were hoping to pick up a bit more knowledge. Then he turned to me and said,

"And perhaps you can tell us Pete, what the hell an ICC is."

Christ All-bloody-mighty! Here I am, £136 worse off, wasting what should have been my last weekend gazing into Beth's greeny-blue eyes and a senior RYA Yachtmaster Instructor doesn't know what an ICC is. Hang on a mo, don't be so stupid Marsh. This is part of my test. He's started already, the crafty sod.

"An International Certificate of Competence, John. As you know."

"And what's one of them, when it's at home?"

I was right, he didn't know.

"Well, it's a sort of International Driver's Licence for yotties. I need one because next week I'm taking my yacht to a lake in France and it's obligatory to have an ICC for inland waters in France. Y'know?"

He didn't, but we'd spend the weekend learning together, John and me. The people at Plas Menai had put a note next to my name, 'Wants ICC', as well as a copy of the test itself (I had my own), and John seemed as determined as I that I should get it. He studied the test and pronounced that it all seemed very straight-forward. I drew his attention to one item, to the effect that I had to be aware that the laws of the country in which one was yottin' had to be carried aboard one's vessel and told him of my letter from CSRIN and the photocopied sheets of laws. I didn't tell him that I intended chartering though, that tit-bit was on a 'need-to-know' basis, but he put a tick against the question anyway. I was off to a flying start!

The others all went off to The Pink Palace for various glasses of assorted liquid and I headed for The Garddfon. I was hoping that Gaz would be in as there were a couple of questions I wasn't sure of on the test and I knew he'd be able to sharpen me up. A month I'd had and no homework had been done. I'd been too busy rushing round the pubs of Cheshire and studying Beth's eyes to be bothered by a little nonsensical revision. Gaz, sadly, was not at the usual haunt so I repaired to The Palace and re-joined my sailing companions.

The weekend went well, we all got on all right, but by Sunday afternoon I was getting a bit fed up with Terry and Sue's incredible habit of telling the same story simultaneously. Jason and Victoria I warmed to, we swopped information about each others' yachts and such. But the real star was Skipper John. I was to learn from Gaz, who turned up in Caernarfon with Plas Menai Paul and Jane on the Saturday night, that he comes from a family history of sailing square-riggers and the like — quite a character.

The high spot for me came on Sunday morning. We'd left Caernarfon with me at the helm and John said he'd point out a mooring he wanted me to pick up.

We arrived and I circled the buoy but there was no pick-up on it.

"OK. So now what do you do?" asked John.

"Play Cowboys and Indians?" I ventured.

"Quite correct. Go for'ard and instruct your crew."

I did, then returned to the cockpit, guided the Fulmar up and we picked up the buoy perfectly, looping a mooring line over it and tying off. The others all went below for morning coffee whilst I stayed in the cockpit buffing up on my last few questions in John's Almanac. I also pointed out to John that I was aware of the need to have somebody on watch at all times, one of the things mentioned on my test sheet. He noted my comment.

Five minutes later, he darted past me and fired up the engine. He was laughing hysterically and said,

"That's the finest piece of watch-keeping I've ever seen. Well done, Pete."

"What? What the hell's going on, John?"

"We've lost our mooring. That's it over there."

I looked in the general direction of his pointed finger. We'd dropped the mooring and it was a good hundred yards away.

"Shit," I muttered, half to myself. "Does that mean I've failed?"

"Look, you're doing OK, it's just that you're putting too much trust in your crew. Check everything you ask them to do, never does any harm and gives you peace of mind."

At that moment I knew I was going to get my ICC. I could've kissed him. It was a sound piece of advice too. I learnt a lot that weekend.

So that was that, the final piece of paperwork was on its way to me and I was nearly ready to leave. You will understand, dear reader, that a considerable amount of legwork was carried out by yours truly to reach this stage of *La Bonne Idée*, and I shall tell you all. Read on.

Chapter 5

DON'T DO IT

*In which I tell of my unsuccessful attempts to
get authority to charter, including a visit to
Provence to meet François' family and a
rendezvous with the Maire of Brouville.
I also meet Bruno, the Président of the Club
Nautique de Brouville.*

"Quite frankly, Mr Marsh, of all our European cousins, you've chosen the worst. Spain, fine. Italy, Greece, even Turkey, fine. But France, forget it."

Those words have been ringing in my ears ever since I'd heard them the previous February. They were uttered so very accurately by the Head Honcho at the Yacht Charter Association. He then told me a story which not only made my blood run cold, it turned out to be very accurate, as I heard it again from another very informed source, the British Consulate in Marseille.

An Englishman, some four or five years previously, had taken two sizeable yachts to the South of France and started doing charters, from what I recall, out of Toulon. As he was sailing under the British flag, he assumed that he had immunity from the French authorities. Now assumption is a very dangerous thing, as I've discovered on my long and winding road through life, and this assumption proved to be a tad on the costly side for said English gent. Both his yachts were impounded and he struggled in his attempts to do battle with the French authorities. All to no avail, despite trying to enlist the co-operation of the RYA, the YCA, even the British Consulate, amongst others. Four months went by, then one of his yachts was sold, presumably to a Frenchman at a knockdown price, in order to settle his fine, and he was ordered to sail away from France in the other one, never to return.

A gruesome tale, told to one who had set his stall out to do day charters in France and my apologies to the gentleman concerned if there are any anomalies in his story — I've repeated it very much as it was told to me. My heart goes out to you sir, and I hope my tale will help to even up the balance a bit. Whatever happened to the European Community idea? I'd love to know.

Undeterred, I struggled manfully on.

Some of my yottie pals had muttered something about insurance so I rang my yacht insurance broker and had an off-the-record conversation with him that went something like this.

"Andy, I'm thinking of taking Rip-Rap to the South of France, dumping her in a lake and doing day charters for the grockles. What do you think the insurance company would say?"

"Hmm. Sounds a lovely idea, Pete. I'm really quite jealous. Don't know. Let me put the feelers out. I'll come back to you."

A few days later I received a letter from him saying roughly, 'no problem, as long as I carried all necessary safety equipment and local licence requirements would be complied with. I was to be on board as skipper at all times and the extra premium for carrying a maximum of four fare-paying people for the season May-September would be £26.28.'

That was one hurdle cleared. I paid the extra premium and put the letter to one side.

It was some days later, when tidying up my kitchen table and filing away important things, that I glanced at the letter again. 'Local licence requirements' were the words that jumped off the page. I rang François, but to no avail. I couldn't understand much of what his wife said, all I could gather was that he wasn't there. No matter, I'd write to him.

Back in January, to celebrate the Big Knob's birthday, Gaz, Beth and I flew EasyJet from Liverpool to Nice and took a long weekend in Cannes and I'd taken them to see Brouville and Le Lac. At that time it was the plan that Gaz would join me on the mammoth journey across France and help with the dumping of Rip-Rap in the lake, so it was necessary for him to see it. Any excuse! They were over-awed and we took many photos which were shown around at the WANCA do in March. Beth had taken a magnificent panoramic view of the lake with Gaz and I to one side and I had taken one of her sitting on a wall outside a house called 'Beth'. But there was no sign of François and the Café du Soleil was firmly shut. At that time it would only have been a courtesy visit anyway, now it was becoming imperative that I enlist the help of the small but beautifully formed Frenchman. A few days after I'd posted my letter to him the phone rang and I picked it up.

"Hello, Peter Marsh," I said, as I always do.

"Hello Peetair Marsh. Eet ees François."

Brilliant. He'd responded at last.

Then I found out why the curious silence and why he hadn't been in Brouville for so long. His father had died after a long illness. I commiserated with him, but he was cheerfully philosophical about the whole thing. Then we got round to my letter and he thought it would be imperative for me to go to Brouville and meet with the *Maire*. He would fix a *rendezvous*. I rang back a few days later and he gave me a date for the following week. EasyJet were doing all right out of me — I'd even remembered the bookings telephone number.

There's one thing I really love about EasyJet and I first encountered it back in September when I'd flown to Nice from Luton for the Cartoon Festival. Arriving quite late at the airport I'd decided not to eat there but wait until I was on the plane. Unlike most people I can put up with the tasteless, plastic splodge that passes for airline food and is dumped in front of you by stewardesses. It's probably something to do with my non-existent taste buds. However, settling down for the take-off, I start to read the in-flight magazine and my eye is drawn to two slogans, one on the front cover, one above the in-flight bar list. On the front cover it says, *'EasyJet's only freebie'* and on the bar list page *'There's no such thing as a free lunch, so we don't give you one'*. My kind of airline!

Mind you, by the time Flight No. EZY 203 glided up to the disembarkation platform at Nice that first time I could have gnawed both hind legs off the proverbial donkey, but it taught me a lesson.

Because of my altercation with Lo-Cost Rent-a-Car and Visa, when we visited Nice in January we'd hired a car from Avis and put it on Gazzer's card. It would've been imprudent to even attempt to use my card, or my name for that matter. I was quite convinced that I had some kind of criminal record in France. We had put a toe in the water and included my name as a second driver. No alarm bells rung and nothing untoward happened in the intervening period.

I was, however, not having had any such thing as a free lunch, in possession of a stomachful of butterflies as I stepped up to the Avis desk at Nice airport that afternoon. Presenting my Driver's Licence, Passport and First Direct credit card, (so prudently applied for and granted around the time my dispute with Visa started) I was, minutes later, handed the keys to a Renault Twingo. The Avis chap was somewhat perplexed when I asked him if it was green, but he shrugged his shoulders and assured me that it was purple. Phew!

"I hate waiting," François hissed through clenched teeth.
So do I.
We're the same star sign, François and I, and I'm a firm believer that there is quite a lot to do with our destinies going on up there somewhere. We were standing in the Mairie de Brouville, the Town Hall if you will. It's nothing more than a converted two-up, two-down town house, but big enough for the day-to-day politics of a small Commune like Brouville to be sorted out in. Trouble is there's nowhere to sit and we've been waiting well over half an hour. To while away the time I show François some of the photos we'd taken in January, particularly the panoramic with Gaz and me on and he lets out a whistle.
"I would like zis one."
"You would? Why? You see this view every day, for real."
"Yes, but see 'ere," he points to a roof at the extreme left of the view, "zis is ze Café du Soleil," then to a wall at the far right, partially obscured by Gaz and I, "and zis 'ere. My 'ouse."
Would you believe it, Gaz and I had been standing right next to

François' house and never known.

I explained that they were Beth's photos, but it planted a seed in my mind.

That morning I'd got up very early, pulled on a tatty pair of jeans and an old sweater, the kind of clothes I feel most comfortable in, and gone for a long, thoughtful walk around Villecroze, the village I'd reached when tiredness and hunger had finally overcome me on the previous evening's drive from Nice. I really didn't know what the gist of my meeting with the *Maire* would be. I had a fair idea of what I wanted but did not know what the reaction to my idea would be. François had been very positive on the phone, but then that's his nature, cocky little chap.

In France, the *Maire* wields great power within the area he holds jurisdiction over. At the end of the day, if he says 'yes', it happens and if he says 'no', it doesn't. I took breakfast of freshly squeezed orange juice, coffee and *croissants* at the hotel, dressed smartly, but casually, a Rip-Rap polo shirt, matching dark blue slacks and black Chelsea boots, then set off for Brouville.

As promised François was waiting for me outside the *Mairie*, dressed in tattered jeans and a sweater with holes in. On his feet were a pair of mud-stained work boots. He assured me that he was coming in with me to speak with the *Maire* and I did wonder what the *Maire* would be wearing. As he came downstairs from his office and apologised for the delay, my question was answered — tattered jeans and a sweater with holes in. The backless clogs had seen better days too. I shouldn't have bothered changing.

All in all the meeting went well, to a point. The whole exercise, however, was in extreme jeopardy and I felt a trifle down as François and I walked up to his house where he'd invited me to meet his family and have lunch. In essence the *Maire* was on my side, he could see the potential in having such a tourist attraction which might draw people to Brouville who might not otherwise visit the village. I'd shown him a proof of the poster I'd designed and said I intended putting these up at campsites situated at the northern end of the lake, near the Gorge. There were stumbling blocks, however.

First, and most importantly, I was not allowed to live aboard

Rip-Rap on the lake. It was explained to me that the water was owned by EDF, the French electricity authority, who laid the law down and no camping was allowed around the perimeter of the lake. That included the pontoon at Brouville. The previous year a young couple had tried it on somebody else's boat but someone had grassed them to *les flics* and off they went, minus a considerable number of *francs*. I could, however, live in a caravan at the Camping Municipal. He offered it to me at the knock-down rate of 1500FF per month (about £150). That was a severe financial setback.

The pontoon would cost 1500FF for a year, I already knew that, I'd found out the previous September. Now I was going to have to find at least another £150 per month for every month I was here and have the added disadvantage of travelling half way round the south end of the lake and back, to and from Le Camping. Also, he wanted to charge me £50 for use of the *poubelles* (dustbins to you and me). That was a trifle in the overall scheme of things. My beloved Evinrude 5hp engine, the little darling that had pulled me out of such scrapes as the one in Moelfre, would have to go and be replaced with a pansy little electric affair, another regulation imposed by the EDF (as the French swop letters around, like VAT becomes TVA, I've done the same and had started to call the EDF rules Effin' EDicts).

Rules are made to be broken and the French make them up by the minute. There are so many and such complex rules I don't think any one Frenchman can possibly know them all. Not even a roomful of Frenchmen. Or a Town Hall full of them. Perhaps, when you are born in France you are entrusted with a rule to remember all your life. That sounds about right — there are 60 million French people in France. No, two rules each. Perhaps three. And oh, by the way, they are allowed to break them, but not Johnny Foreigner, no bloody chance. Even if you're doing something right they'll make up a rule that says it isn't right and entrust it to yet another new-born. Then fine you and, if you're lucky, deport you. If you're unlucky, they sling you in jail, in a stinking windowless cell with the rule book, which you must learn by heart before you can be released. And, as the daily supplement of new rules is posted through the slot at the bottom of the door (normally reserved for your daily bread and water) the task becomes a daunting one.

Then came le crunch. Maire Duchatel put his pen down and removed his spectacles.

You will have to register your activities with the *Société des Métiers* in the county town, he explained. That's a sort of register for self-employed folk who want to work in France. Then get *Assurances*, but not the insurance I'd got. I showed him my certificate that I'd got from the brokers with the clause about day charters highlighted in yellow and he nodded in assent, but then explained that I would have to pay the equivalent of our National Insurance as well as all the taxes, local and national. And then, I'd have to write to the *Prefect de Police* for his permission. That was the easy bit, merely a formality because he, the *Maire*, has approved my scheme.

He picked up his pen and wrote it all out for me. I took the piece of paper, thanked him, shook him by the hand and followed François out of the office.

"I don't know François. It all sounds very complicated to me."

We were walking up the steep narrow street to his house.

"Peetair, you worry too much."

"Bloody right I do pal. This is a minefield and I don't know the way out."

"No, zis is zee road to my 'ouse. I know ze way."

"You don't understand, *mon ami*. There is so much red tape, so many formalities. And I'm English. I don't think I'm going to be too popular with the other people trying to fleece the tourists who come to Brouville."

"But zis is zee way eet ees done *en France*. Zee regulations."

"Perhaps I could do it as part of your business, the Café. That's it, we do an all-in price to include an afternoon's yottin' and a slap-up meal at Chez François. How about that?"

The smile was benign, the answer wasn't.

"Impossible, my friend. In France zis ees impossible."

DON'T DO IT!

It was many months later that I found out the reason why. Unlike England, where you simply set up a business, any kind of business and register with the Inland Revenue as self employed, in France you have to specifically register the precise nature of your business. Owning and running a café as a business does not include offering water-borne jollies around the pond. All François can do is sell food and drink. True socialism at work. *Fin.* End of story.

"Allo everybodee."

The greeting came from a curious mouth with enormous buck teeth. In fact the whole face reminded me of Bugs Bunny, but instead of whiskers, this one had a very French droopy moustache and the face was in the airing cupboard and the airing cupboard was in the roof.

Now in England access to an airing cupboard is usually at floor or waist height. Judging by the items surrounding the face this was an airing cupboard and it was definitely in the roof. There was a ladder reaching up to the face and the face belonged, I was told by François, to Bruno, *le Président du Club Nautique de Brouville*. These two had done all the renovations to François' house and he was showing me proudly around. François was the brains, I was told, Bruno the skills. A bit like me and Roge, I suppose. I do have to say though, they've done a great job. It's a smashing little place.

From the tiled entrance hall, flanked by two bedrooms, one for each of the children François and his wife have made (his words), there leads a stairway to the first floor. It emerges in a very French kitchen, huge uneven floor tiles, heavy deal furniture and a collection of Le Creuset pots and pans that Harrods would be proud to put on display. The beamed ceiling is festooned with bunches of dried herbs and flowers, strings of garlic and the like, creating an aroma and look which could only be Provence. Balancing the kitchen and about the same size is the lounge, sparsely but neatly furnished. Up another flight of stairs is the master bedroom, en-suite, but as yet incomplete, and through the window, a magnificent view of the lake. Now I knew why

François wanted Beth's panoramic pic.

"Allo everybodee."

The greeting I would get to know and love was issued forth once more and Bruno descended the ladder, offering me his hand. It's a curious handshake — a claw is extended well before it arrives at touching distance. Then it does briefly squeeze before diving into a trouser pocket and emerging with a packet of fags. He lit up and we descended the stairs to the kitchen, François first, then Bruno, and I followed in a cloud of Gitanes smoke. I was then introduced to the family, who'd arrived back from school for the lunchbreak. Katrine, François' lovely Dutch wife, Sadie and Jules, his children — a perfectly delightful family of which François is rightfully very proud.

"No. I will do it!"

François brushed Katrine to one side and took over the food prep. I showed her the photos whilst Bruno busied himself with pouring the *pastis*. She was very taken with the snap of Beth and 'Beth' and, in truth, Katrine reminded me very much of Beth. The same build, height and posture, an open, smiling face which puts you instantly at ease. One major difference — Katrine has very blonde, almost white hair and Beth's is jet black.

"*Très jolie*," she said, and I puffed up with pride.

"*Et vous Katrine, la même-chose.*"

I indicated the face and eyes, and the figure. She burst into peels of laughter and said '*non*' repeatedly. Honestly, the modesty of some women. Why can't they just accept that they're attractive?

Bruno thrust a glass of *pastis* into my hand and I sipped it whilst watching François in his culinary efforts at the cooker. A rapid-fire conversation was going on between the men and I tried to understand the gist of it all.

From what I could gather, François was telling Bruno of my plans and our meeting with the *Maire*. I pulled my photos of Rip-Rap out of my briefcase and spread them on the table for Bruno to see. He picked them up one by one and studied them carefully. He knew his yachts, I could tell instantly. He spotted the roller-reefing genoa, the lazy-jacks and admired her lines. Then he picked up the shot of her on the trailer. I'd brought that one along to show the *Maire* and ask him, if my project was to go ahead, if there was anywhere I could store the trailer for the summer and the boat on the trailer for the winter, if all was successful and I was to return and repeat the venture the following year. He had shrugged and suggested either Le Camping or perhaps *le Club Nautique*, and here was *le Président* of same sitting across le deal table.

Bruno studied this photo closely and then asked about the keel arrangement. I explained that it was a skeg keel with a pivoting drop centreboard and he nodded his approval. I rather gather he said, 'perfect for the lake'.

"*Très joli*," he said, putting the last photo down on the table and collecting them up like a pack of cards. "*Très joli*."

So that was that. I had a *joli* boat and a *jolie* girlfriend and I was about to have a *joli* lunch.

I'd been half watching François as he prepared the food.

He'd sliced a *baguette* up into thickish chunks, placed a huge dollop of cheese on each slice, covered the whole lot with herbs, olives and slices of beef tomato, then liberally sprinkled the ensemble with olive oil before placing the baking tray in the top oven. Now he sat at the table with us and we attacked a salami style of thing that he'd brought from his recent weekend skiing trip in the Alps. I'd learned about this little jaunt when we'd arranged my visit to the *Maire*, and he now regaled us with stories of the trip. It had been taken to celebrate his best friend's 50th, a lads' weekend, it seems, and he saved the juicy bits until Katrine got up from the table and took the children back to school. She returned as François put the baking tray of goodies on the table and told me that it was 'cheese of the *chèvre*'. I'd actually guessed as much because there are a lot of *Fromage de Chèvre* farms in Provence. Goat's milk cheese. Katrine got up and went for her French-English dictionary as I explained to François that I understood, it was goat's milk cheese.

"The she-goat!" Katrine exclaimed.

So I said,

"Of course — you wouldn't get much milk from a he-goat, now would you."

69

They laughed, thankfully.

As we devoured this excellent, yet simple repast, the subject of my project came up once more. Bruno said I'd have to get a Skipper's licence and I told him that it was a mere formality. I'd go to the National Watersports Centre at Plas Menai and get it. (Little did I know at that time!). Bruno nodded his approval.

Then there was the matter of my registering at the *Société des Métiers*. Could they tell me where it was as I could go there on my way back to Nice? I was worried about my lack of French for this task but was hoping that someone there would speak English. After all, there are loads of English workers in Provence. Then things really looked up. Bruno was going to the county town to pick up his daughter from college and was leaving in ten minutes. I could follow him and he would go with me and explain my requirements to them. Brilliant. I bade a hasty goodbye to François and Katrine and followed Bruno.

We parked right outside the *Métiers* office and went in. Bruno explained the situation but they said '*non*', and suggested we try the *Chambre de Commerce*. So we went there. '*Non*', what we wanted was the *Affaires Maritime* in Toulon.

Out on the sun-baked pavement I thanked Bruno and made to leave. His daughter Sandra arrived and we were introduced. Then I said goodbye and got into the Twingo. I waved as I left and felt a twinge in my back, not a very painful one, but a familiar one. I headed towards Toulon, but as I approached the Autoroute the pain had started to increase. I knew just what it was, pleurisy. I've had it before.

My quest would have to be put on hold for a while but I had the address and telephone number of the *Affaires Maritime* and was certain I could handle it all from England. The Twingo turned towards Nice and home.

The light was blinking on my Ansaphone as I walked through the cottage door a week or so later. The pleurisy had been quickly abated by a course of antibiotics and I'd spent some time on the phone, largely getting nowhere. I went over to the instrument and pressed the 'start' button. The dulcet tones of a Scotsman issued forth from the speaker.

"Hulloo, Mr Marsh, Stuart MacFarlane here from the British Embassy in Paris. Just replying to the message you left on my voice mail earlier. I hope we can make contact the next time. Goodbye."

I rifled through a sheaf of papers on my desk, my file on the project, found his direct line number and dialled it.

I'd been put on to the dulcet Mr MacFarlane by a chap at the *Affaires Maritime* in Brest. I'd been put onto them by the *Chambre de Commerce de France en Angleterre* in London, and put on to them by the French Consulate in London, who, it had been suggested to me by the *Affaires Maritime* in Toulon, might be able to help. What the dulcet one was about to suggest caused me to reach for the Scotch bottle, a singularly apposite way of dealing with the situation.

"I'd suggest the *Affaires Maritime* people in Toulon. They'd be ye best bet."

Now I have to confess that I hadn't explained the whole story to Mr MacFarlane, to have done so would have perhaps doubled the number of Euros already spent with BT on this project alone. I was keeping it more and more economical in outlining exactly what it was I wanted to achieve. He didn't know that they had been the third port of call in this farcical round robin, until now that was.

I did then explain, as briefly as I could, who I'd spoken to, what they'd said and how I ended up speaking to him. I finished up by making some comment about how difficult it must be for him having to deal with French bureaucracy.

"It is Mr Marsh, believe me it is. I came here from a small South American country so obscure you will not have heard of it, which is controlled alternatively by a military junta and a band of blood-thirsty guerrillas. Life there was simple compared to here!"

Anyway it looked as if things were going to move on. He promised to get a chap called Joe to ring me from the British Consulate in Marseille who he was sure would be able to help me. He promised to brief Joe fully so that if for any reason I had to ring him back the call would at least be a shortish one. I thanked him and wished him better luck with his next posting.

Joe did indeed ring me a couple of days later and reiterated the tale of the Englishman and his confiscated yachts. Then he suggested I ring a chap called Johann at someplace I didn't catch the name of, but it was in Marseille and Joe was certain that he was the man for me. I did and Johann promised he would put my dilemma to his Regional Delegate. I thanked him and totally forgot about the conversation. The world had gone mad and was threatening to take me with it.

This was about the time of the WANCAs launching weekend at the end of March and to be truthful, I'd just decided to go to France and try to muddle my way through all the red tape when I got there. The departure date was a week away when I received that letter from the CSRIN in Marseille, accompanied as it was by all the yottin' laws of France. It was signed by the Regional Delegate, one Gil Perrion. Johann had done his stuff despite the fact that it had taken M. Perrion over two months to write the letter. 'Mañana' doesn't only happen in Spain, you know.

I read the letter excitedly, my French is not good, but the gist of the letter was that I could do it, if I registered my activities, had the necessary *Assurances*, a Skipper's licence and I could sail under the British flag. Brilliant. All I had to do was go back to the *Société des Métiers*, show them this letter and surely then they would take me on. Everything else I had, including the red duster. Well almost. The ICC was on its way and Mother promised to forward it to me at the Café du Soleil as soon as it arrived. I'd rented out my cottage and all my mail was being re-directed to Mother anyway, so it would soon arrive.

Yippee, *la belle France*, here we come!

Chapter 6

JUST DO IT!

*In which I tell of the preparations for my
adventure, leaving home and the journey.
The campsite where I was to live and the
campsite receptionist, Martine. The launch of
Rip-Rap and my first taste of lake yottin',
as well as more tales of my struggle
to get permission to charter.*

I adjusted the cap and admired myself in the sports shop mirror. A dark blue Nike cap, with the 'tick' logo emblazoned in white on the front. Very smart, but not my favourite cap, the one I'd used for yottin' these past ten or so years. I'd left that somewhere and couldn't track it down. So this was to be its replacement and dark blue to match the rest of the Rip-Rap sports and leisurewear. Rugby shirts for the racing crew and polo shirts for shore wear, posing around yacht clubs and the like, all embroidered with the Rip-Rap namestyle in red. I'd had these made up before the launch and doled them out to the deserving, and very smart they look too.

The particularly pleasing one is the rugby shirt worn by Chrissie, a stunningly attractive blonde whose father won the Fastnet Race some years back. I'd been trying to get Chrissie to come yottin' with me for some time. She told me she was only interested in racing, so I gave her the rugby shirt for her 21st birthday and she promised to come with us for Celtic Race Week. As Chrissie works behind the bar of my favourite local hostelry and her father also frequents the place, it gives me great pleasure to watch his face as he seethes when she wears it. It also gives Chrissie much pleasure too, winding her father up. Celtic Week took place whilst her parents were away on holiday so they don't actually know whether Chrissie was with us or not, and if she's not telling then I'm certainly not. Its also one in the eye for the drinking buddies who take the mickey out of me — they don't know for sure either. You see, Chrissie missed her shifts behind the bar that week and speculation ran, and still runs, high.

As previously stated, I'm not one for detailed preparation, I rather hope that things will just happen, so the last few days before departure were hectic. Rip-Rap was ready but I was not. I'd dipped in and out of doing jobs all winter, so she was ready. The bottom rubbed down and anti-fouled, the Solar Battery Charger rigged up, complete with voltmeter and a real Tillatenda fitted. The bodge job I'd done in Barmouth turned out to be woefully inadequate, never actually working when I really needed it to. The damn thing got me into more trouble than if I'd never had it. Gaz had told me where to get a real one, through a mail order place. He'd also suggested that I strip the cockpit duck boards and seats, which were varnished, and oil them instead. The fierce sun of the S of F he said would burn the varnish off in no time flat, so I'd done as he said. Looks well too.

The trailer was also given a dose of looking at, I was none too sure of the brakes. I'd had a lurid moment in Knutsford on the way back from the Straits last October, so I had my man Steve give them the once over. He also gave the ageing Volvo a thorough service and I signed up for the AA Five Star Service. The French Consulate had sent me a comprehensive pack of information regarding driving through France and I'd spent some time planning my best route and working out how much toll money I would need for the Autoroutes. I also discovered that one could stay free overnight at the many lay-by and picnic areas they have beside the Autoroutes, so that was the plan.

A visit to Halfords was in order, to purchase a reflective triangle and spare set of bulbs for the car, both obligatory in France. I also bought a set of headlamp deflectors and, because I'd spent more than £15, I got a free Road Atlas of Europe worth £8.99. To round off the vehicular side of things, I paid a call to the insurance brokers to organise a green card. Transpires you can only get one for three months of the year and as I was going to be away for four, this was no good.

The broker suggested a master stroke. On the day my three

months was up he'd swop insurance companies, write me out a cover note, apply for a new green card to run from the first day of the new cover and post everything off to me. Then, on my return to England we could cancel the green card and I'd still have two months left for the start of next summer's adventure, doing the same thing next year. Brilliant. There was just one thing I'd overlooked, car tax, but I'll come to that shortly.

Then I had to get myself organised, a million and one things to attend to and so little time. An E111 medical form was obtained from the Post Office and I invested in a first aid kit and some other medications I most frequently use, paracetamol, kaolin and morphine, that sort of thing.

An abundance of food supplies was laid in, tins of beans, pasta spirals and the like, coffee, dried milk, sugar and three beef-in-ale pies, Luke's favourite. Despite not having an oven aboard Rip-Rap I was sure the caravan would have one, so we could feast ourselves when he came to visit me.

I packed on the day before departure, T-shirts, knickers and shorts, in the main. One group of items I did pack and spent the summer marvelling at my gross stupidity for, was thermal yottin' socks. God alone knows why I packed them, but I did. I suppose that mentally I was going on an extended yottin' trip, so the socks had to go in. I also took the three full sets of off-shore oilies which I normally keep on board during the English summer and three pairs of yottin' wellies. Daft bugger. I'd been in France almost exactly a month when we had our first shower, and that's all it was, a shower. Mind you, when it did eventually rain it came down in lumps; you'll hear about that later.

So, I was largely ready to go and I'd rung Gaz to tell him. He suggested an early doors drink at The Bull's Head, a hostelry we frequent near my mother's house, where I'd be spending my last night. We left Macclesfield, Rip-Rap and I, and headed for Northwich. No lurid braking incidents through Knutsford this time, but just on the other side I was flashed by somebody coming in the other direction and again from behind. I pulled over and the car behind skidded to a dramatic halt. A yuppie jumped out clutching his mobile phone and whimpered,

"Something's just fallen off your trailer and hit my car."
I looked at the front of his car and it seemed OK.
"What colour was it, this thing?" I asked.
"White. Why?"

I looked up at where the mast lay on top of the boat and spotted that the piece of thick foam I use on top of the coachroof to stop the mast vibrating had gone missing. Can't have secured it too well, if at all. Amazing what you forget. The yuppie was punching a number into his mobile and I suddenly realised he wasn't ringing his wife to tell her that he was in his car and on the way home. He was ringing the police. I grabbed the instrument from him and switched it off.

"It was a piece of foam rubber, you toss-pot. There's no damage to your car whatsoever. Now bugger off."

I handed the phone back to him and amazingly he did bugger off. I glanced back down the road and saw a police Range-Rover pull up and the driver throw my precious piece of foam into the ditch. I legged it back to retrieve the foam as the Range-Rover sped past. He could've brought it to me, they are after all our servants. We pay their wages, don't we?

I told this tale in The Bull's Head that night, to great merriment and mirth.

"Typical," said Gaz. "You've only had the best part of six months preparing for this trip and you forget something as basic as that."

I was a bit hurt, it'd been a hectic few days and that had been the last in a lot of preparatory jobs. I never forgot to do it again, even though, each night of the journey I had to move the mast in order to gain access to the cabin.

All my family were there, as well as Beth and a few WANCAs. Despite not being able to join me for the journey for too many complex reasons which I won't bore you with, Gaz had rung round and Tim, Dunc and his brother Paul attended the send-off.

Whilst parking up on a car park near Mother's house where I'd arranged to leave Rip-Rap overnight, I'd pulled all the wires out of the trailer light socket and asked Tim if there was any set sequence for replacing them. He said there must be and maybe they were marked inside the socket itself. Failing that, it'd be trial and error. Brother Nico had obviously over-heard this conversation, but not said anything, for some half an hour after my family had left he returned and threw me a brand new socket still in its packaging, and on the back, a full set of wiring instructions.

"Found it in the garage," was all he said.

That would save me at least an hour's messing about in the morning.

For some reason, Nico has always been like that with me. Although we have a quiet relationship in terms of seeing each other, talking on the phone and such, there is a great love between us and whenever possible we both go out of each other's way to help if we can.

There was nothing anybody could help me with on the next day's problem, taxing the car.

I'd had it MoT'd the previous day but purposely left taxing it to the last minute thinking I could simply go into a post office and get a new disc — the current one was due to expire at the end of June. So having fixed the new plug to the trailer, I wandered down to the post office with Mother. She wanted her pension and knew the ladies behind the counter very well, but there was nothing they could do. They hadn't been issued with the next months' discs and wouldn't be until the 18th. It was the 11th. They rang Chester and sure enough I'd have to go to the VRO there. I un-hitched the trailer, set off and did the deed, then returned to Mother's.

"What are you doing here?" I smiled down at the lovely face and beautiful greeny-blue eyes.

"Just popped by to see your Mum and saw Rip-Rap was still here".

The three of us went off for a pub lunch and two big hugs later I was waving farewell to the two women I love the most.

Mind-blowingly boring is the only way I can describe motorway or Autoroute driving when you're towing the best part of three and half tons. Interspersed that is, with tense moments of abject terror.

We'd made it as far as Maidstone Services and I was knackered. I pulled in and positioned the rig as best I could. I was actually beginning to feel like an HGV driver, having spent so much time that day surrounded by them, so from now on I shall describe my ensemble as 'the rig'. Sustenance was taken and I noted that there was a Travel Shop here that would open at 7 o'clock in the morning and I could buy Ferry tickets. I'd purposely not booked anything so as not to put any undue pressure on myself with having to make deadlines. This, after all was supposed to be my holiday, until I started chartering anyway. Also, arriving at Dover with a ticket would see me straight through to the embarkation area.

The day dawned. I wandered over for a trukkies scram and bought my tickets. The lady was not at all busy so we spent a while working out the cheapest option for my requirements. She also gave me a GB sticker for the trailer, nice lady. The AA Five Star do-dah, despite reminding you that 'if towing a trailer, you must ensure that a GB sticker is also attached to the trailer', only contains one. Take note. These are all good tips for any reader who may be contemplating such an ordeal as mine.

I covered the forty or so miles to Dover in less than an hour and pulled into the allocated embarkation lane — it was with the trucks, of course. I lit up and made small talk with the other trukkies as we waited to be called for embarkation. That done I made my way upstairs to the bar.

One pint of Guinness was all I allowed myself and then to the duty-free shop. Tobacco and camera film for me, whisky for François and Bruno, a litre of Johnny Walker Black Label. All those months ago, when Bruno and I were trying to get me registered for business, I'd opened my briefcase for something and he'd spotted a bottle of D-F whisky I had therein. His usually popped-out eyes popped out even further and I heard him mutter 'Aaah, whiskee' from somewhere under his moustache. It had been noted and here was the boys' reward for all the help they had and were going to give me.

I had heard some spooky stories about having your boat in

France without all the correct documentation. The man at the YCA had told me a couple, so I was well prepared with a file containing my SSR licence and the Title Deeds to Rip-Rap declaring that I had paid VAT in England. The fact that the previous boat name appeared on this document didn't bother me, as I'd also taken a letter from the boatyard in which it mentioned Rip-Rap as being my vessel. It would surely be no problem for me to explain that I'd simply changed the name. Also the radio licence which she had for '96/7 with the original name on it was still attached to one of the cabin windows and I'd never bothered removing it.

I'd taken the radio off and left it in England though, as I was unsure of French regulations regarding the use of these things and I was unlikely to hear 'Rip-Rap, Rip-Rap, Rip-Rap. This is Rufus, Rufus. Come in please.'

My worries were unfounded however — the French *douanes* appeared to be out to lunch as the rig sailed through disembarkation and out onto the Autoroute.

More mind-blowingly boring miles, but this time they were kilometres, so they were eaten up faster. My plan to stop over at the lay-bys did not appeal one little bit. I stopped at one to stretch my legs and there didn't seem to be anything other than a toilet block there. I also had a disturbing feeling of loneliness and felt that I could be the target of a gang of heavily-armed French thugs trying to make off with my pride and joy. And me in it!

The regular service station places also looked out of the question — they would be very noisy with *camions* pulling in and out all night and I didn't fancy the entertainment facilities much. The night spent at Maidstone had put me off this idea.

I did, however, have a strange encounter at the first Autoroute fuel stop. I'd tanked up the rig, gone into the shop to pay and was just returning, tucking away credit card, receipt and all, when a female grabbed my arm and a strident Aussie voice cut the airwaves.

"Hey cobber, we use four star in the UK. Wha'd'yer put in here?"

"Super."

"What's with you pommie bastards? Everything's bloody super, fantastic, got-to-believe-it, gosh. What fucking gas do I put in my car, for chrissakes?"

"Super." I led her gently to the rank of fuel pumps and pointed to the red one, the one marked 'Super'. "There. Super. Right?"

"Oh! Yeah. Hey sorry, didn't understand. Must be your accent, or something."

"Could be," I replied, smiling. "See you."

"I doubt it," came the almost inaudible reply, made through clenched teeth.

I journeyed on, left the Autoroute at Sommesous and made my way south to the town of Troyes. On the outskirts of the town I saw a sign for the Camping Municipal and turned in. £6 for the night and a relatively secure environment in which to leave the rig and walk into town for a beer or two. I locked up and made my way to the campsite entrance. On the way, I spied a very familiar looking, British registered, silver Ford Escort and paused to look again. Peering at me through the obviously camp-owned caravan window was an even more familiar face, the Aussie chick.

"Hi, Helen," I shouted, and waved. The face disappeared from the window and then re-appeared at the door.

"Who the fuck are you calling Helen? It's Kylie!"

"Sorry, old thing. We weren't introduced, formally. Helen. Of Troyes. Thought it suited you."

"Fuck off, you pommie bastard!"

"Super," I said.

The very first time I encountered an Australian girl was in a pub in Earl's Court somewhere in the middle of the Sixties. I was rather taken aback by her response to my question as to how come she was over here, in England?

"It was my Dad's idea," she said. "'Gilly, my girl,' he said, 'yer sittin' on a fortune. Spread yer legs and go see the world.' So I did."

That was the Swinging Sixties and I was in London, but I was only 21 at the time and my public school education hadn't prepared me for female Aussie banter and I've been a little nervous of it ever since. However, Helen of Troyes' little tit-bit wasn't to be the last of female Aussie repartee I would hear that summer, as you'll discover.

Walking into town, I was reminded that something called the World Cup was on. Could I find a quiet bar? No bloody chance, and something else I've pondered on in one of my many pondering moments: why, when England hosted the European Cup was it called Euro 96 and now, when France were hosting the World Cup was it called France 98? Typical Gallic arrogance was my thought at the time and I shall cover this subject in a later chapter, but I do have to say in retrospect it was their year to win the thing, so fair enough.

It's not to say they're all arrogant, far from it.

The very next day, as the rig trundled across the southern bit of northern France, the old tummy started rumbling and I realised it needed something solid inside it. A quick glance at the Road Atlas of Europe and a double check with the road signs, confirmed that I was nearing the ancient towns of Nuits-St-George and Gevrey Chambertin, known by all wine appreciating WANCAs as Geoffrey Chamber-Tin. Now the latter was some way north of the former and would mean a double back of 20 miles or so for the rig, so the former was selected and we rolled into the town square of Nuits-St-George, a pretty little town, beautifully kept and looking quite delightful in the early afternoon sun, but nowhere to park the rig, at least nowhere obvious. I stopped outside a very up-market *Cave*, selling a very up-market selection of grape juice, judging by the prices on the sandwich board, the view of which I'd just obscured from the passing traffic. In fact the rig obscured most of the front of the *Cave*, but I went in anyway.

The chap inside was delightful, came outside, admired Rip-Rap and said in perfect English that it was possible for me to leave her there for an hour whilst I went to quieten the rumblings. All he did was move the afore-mentioned sandwich board round to the road side of the rig. He bowed courteously, smiled and wished me *'Bon appetit'*.

ROUND AND ROUND IN CIRCLES

An hour later I returned and went back into the *Cave*, in order to ask the nice man to move his sandwich board, but I couldn't leave without purchasing something, could I? A deal was done on half a case of *Beaujolais Villages*, the nice man moved his sandwich board and returned to his many customers. It seemed that Rip-Rap had caused quite some interest and he'd spent the last hour dragging people off the pavement and into his *Cave*. The enterprising fellow also got a sale out of me, so all in all, a good hour. I'll go there again.

The sense of security I'd had the previous night spent at the Camping Municipal had decided me to do the same again, so that evening I turned off the Autoroute and headed for a town called Vienne. I soon saw the familiar sign with the wigwam and caravan on it, indicated left and made the turn. The next ten minutes were to be the most terrifying of the journey.

It was a narrow, steep hill I'd turned on to, with very tight S-bends. So steep was it that I was forced to shift the Volvo's automatic gearbox down to low. She still only made very slow progress with the engine screaming and nought miles per hour on the speedo. I was some way up this hill before I was able to pull off and let the cars who'd stacked up behind pass me, but there was a way to go yet before I could contemplate turning the rig round and I'd just seen a sign that indicated the Camping to be 12 kilometres away. I did find a farm entrance and judged that this was just wide enough for me to reverse into. It wasn't. Despite my best efforts Rip-Rap clouted a tree. I jumped out in some alarm, fearing what damage I might have done, but it was only superficial. A good rub with T-Cut would bring her up like new.

Slowly back down the hill, still in low gear, but with the brakes constantly applied for fear of the rig running away with itself and I approached the bottom. Here the road levelled out a bit and I took my foot off the brake some 50 yards from the junction. It was a main road I was approaching and they don't have the *'Priorité à droite'* rule any more in France. I passed the *'Cédez le passage'* sign and applied the brakes once more. My foot went down to the floor and if anything the rig seemed to be gathering speed. Nothing.

Absolutely nothing. I sailed gracefully onto the main road, slotting the rig neatly between two speeding *camions*, and continued on my way. For 150 yards that is.

My heart was in my mouth, my stomach felt like a spin drier and the excellent lunch I'd enjoyed in Nuits-St-George threatened to make an involuntary re-appearance. The rig, as luck would have it, found a conveniently placed lay-by and the hand brake was utilised for a gentle stop. I'd had no time to indicate and the *camion* behind was none too pleased, judging by the amount of pressure and length of time that *le trukkie* applied to his *'ootere*, but I cared little. I was still alive and the rig relatively unscathed. The stench of burning brake pads was a trifle unpleasant though, so I rolled a fag and took a short stroll.

My hands had stopped shaking and the clamminess wiped off when I resumed my search for a safe overnight haven fifteen minutes later. As I left the lay-by, having waited for a long gap in the traffic, I gingerly tried the brakes and they seemed to work OK. I travelled slowly though, completely oblivious to the hooting from behind.

The restaurant and bar at that night's Camping was most pleasant. I felt in need of a *pastis* or two after my brakeless incident and I could think of nowhere more pleasant to take the medicine. The liquid aniseed was poured by Ginger Spice and delivered to my table by Posh, Sporty or Scary, whichever happened to be free at the time. No sign of Baby though; is she the one who left? Or is she *'la fiancée de David Beckham'*? I know and care not. I'd come to France to get away from the World Cup and The Spice Girls, but the waitresses in L'Auberge de Bois that evening were doing a very pretty and splendid job.

As I'd walked through the door my eyes were immediately drawn to a roaring log fire. The temperature had been in the early 30's all day according to the electronic signs above the Autoroute, and here we had a log fire. It was some while later, when the first diners arrived that I realised why; *le Patron* cooked on it, and that, presumably was why the establishment was called L'Auberge de Bois. All makes sense eventually.

*

"Jesus Christ! Is this ever going to end?"

The rig bounced and lurched its way along what appeared, on the Road Atlas of Europe anyway, to be a main arterial highway. It was red on the Atlas, very straight and I had thought it'd be something like those roads you see huge trucks thundering along in American movies. I could imagine the rig being tracked by a low flying helicopter with a film camera on board, as the Director shouted instructions to his Cameraman. 'OK, pull out now. Let's go for the wide shot. Its all looking pretty damn smooth down there.' It damn well wasn't.

The last major road building programme to be carried out in France, apart from the Autoroutes that is, was when France was called Gaul and it was undertaken by the Romans. They built long, straight, cobbled roads for their legionnaires to march up and down and, as the Roman Empire was going to last forever, their roads were to last forever also, or so they thought. The French thought so as well apparently, because they've not done much with them this past couple of millennia. Apart, that is from spreading a bit of tarmac around and printing up a lot of yellow and red triangular signs with a black exclamation mark and lettering that says 'Chaussée Deformée'. Forgive me if I've spelt that wrong, there may be one or two 's's and 'e's too many, but it's difficult to focus when your specs are bouncing around on the bridge of your nose.

The Chaussée Deformée I was currently trying to focus on was, as mentioned, a main arterial highway in the Atlas, but in reality, nothing more than a partially tarmaced, partially cobbled farm track, and the rig thundered along it at 80kph, most of the time being spent on the trailer jockey wheel. It'd become a nine-wheeled rig and a damned uncomfortable one to ride in, let alone drive.

All this had come about because Marsh had eventually got bored with Autoroute driving. The gypsy and romantic in him sought adventure, so a quick study of the Road Atlas had led him to believe that, if one turned off the Autoroute at Avignon Sud and headed east for Manosque, one would save 70 or so kilometres and £14 worth of toll money. Damned fool.

Spotting a red traffic light just in time, right in the middle of a town called Apt, the rig screamed to a slithering halt. Well, the tyres and the driver did the screaming, the rig just slithered. It was time for a break, a very apt time.

The rig pulled up in the large town square car park and reversed once more into a tree. The driver slammed the rig door and made off for a beer. Two, in fact. The rig still had nearly 100 kilometres of *Chaussée Deformée* to traverse and some kind of help was required.

It was two and a half hours later when I breasted a hill and looked down at the glistening ribbon stretching along the valley as far as the eye could see. This was the Autoroute I'd abandoned some five hours and several years ago and I still had a steep hill to descend to even get near it. Heart in mouth, I inched the rig forward. The town of Manosque flew by and so did the Autoroute; I crossed it where I should have left it. Surely I was on the last lap. The only real challenge left was the town of Riez.

Gaz, Beth and I had visited Riez in January in order for me to recce the route and I'd spotted a very narrow part of the road, right in the middle of town. Fortunately the arrows on the road signs indicated that the direction I would be travelling in gave me right of way. Remember what I said about how the French make rules up just so that they can break them? This little rule was one of them. The rig was stuck in the middle of said narrow bit for about fifteen minutes whilst an awful lot of shouting and horn blowing went on. Eventually, two nice men in smart blue uniforms came to sort the melée out and, having given the drivers in front of me a right good ticking off and a lot of waggy-finger, they saluted the rig and we left Riez for Brouville.

Breasting yet another hill just south of Pruniers, Rip-Rap got the first glance of her new home. I swear she whinnied, or whatever expression of delight it is that boats make. I certainly did. I could already taste the ice cold beer sitting in front of me on a table outside the Café du Soleil.

The lake looked as good as it always does, its ultra greeny-blue waters glistening in the warm Provençal sun. Until folk actually see it, the Lac de Ste Serre looks like a heavily re-touched postcard, on photographs at least. Its something to do with the limestone or whatever it is that the water travels across on its way to the lake, which is man-made and very, very deep. The day we arrived the Mistral was blowing and there were white horses on the water. It was all positively orgasmic. The arrival in Brouville however wasn't.

I'd telephoned François the day I left England and told him I'd be there on Sunday. I was, he wasn't. The ice cold beer sat on the table in front of me, served very efficiently by a chap who didn't know me from Adam, and I sat in lonely isolation and gazed at it. I was the only customer at the Café du Soleil that afternoon. I hadn't expected bunting and flag-waving folk lining the streets, but I did somehow think François and/or Bruno would be there. I gulped the beer down and ordered another. The waiter disappeared into the Café to do my bidding and I felt a hand on my shoulder.

"Rip-Rap, she is here?"

The beautiful little Frenchman extended his right hand and I grasped it. I pulled myself up and we embraced. Then I was introduced to Milko, the waiter who'd returned with my fresh beer.

"Ah, Peetair. *Oui*, Peetair," was all he said, as we shook hands, but I gathered that François would have told him of my imminent arrival and because I hadn't parked the rig right outside the Café he obviously hadn't realised who I was.

Quite a character is Milko, more of him later.

"Rip-Rap, I can see her?"

"Not from here, but you can from over there," I replied.

"Please?"

"Come with me François."

I took him to the parapet that borders the *boules* pitch and we looked down on the public car park where fifteen minutes earlier the rig had heaved a huge sigh of relief and was now resting.

"She is beautiful."

"Thank you François. I think so too, but right now, not as

beautiful as your beer. Have one with me."

We repaired arm-in-arm to the Café and had several. Then I ordered one of François' Entrecôtes with Roquefort Sauce *avec pommes frites*, and washed the whole lot down with *un demi* of the local red.

I slept very soundly and illegally aboard Rip-Rap that night, on the public car park and for the last time.

"God. It's ghastly." I stepped out of the tiny caravan and looked helplessly at the two women who'd shown me to it.

"Jus' a bit of tidyin' up an' it will be fine," said the one who spoke English.

I'd introduced myself to her in the Camping Municipal reception, in French, and she'd asked me if I spoke English. I'd said 'yes', but she was still convinced I was German.

The caravan measured 3 x 2 metres, it was very old (there were stickers inside dating back to 1968) and it had a cooker but no gas, a sink but no water and for a while at least, one light bulb but no electricity. Oh, and of course, no bog. All these things I have aboard Rip-Rap, and she's a good bit bigger. Four metres bigger in fact, but because of the Effin' EDicts, I was not allowed to live on her. The comment about 'a bit of tidyin' up' caused me to smile as well. I tried, but you'd never know.

I returned to the reception following the two women who gabbled on a bit. I rather gathered that the one who spoke English had only just started and the other one had arrived after a phone call to the *Mairie* pleading for some explanation as to why this German was here demanding a caravan. She'd turned up with a piece of paper which had the *Maire's* stamp and signature on. It informed us that *'Monsieur PETER'* had been allocated said caravan for four months at a monthly rent of 1500FF, my deal with the *Maire*. Quite clear, even I could make that out, but this non-English speaking person couldn't. She was demanding 1500FF up front and a monthly rental of nearly double that amount. She was obviously having trouble with her native language. Transpires she's a school teacher, but nothing about that breed would surprise me. I'd been married to one for nigh on fifteen years.

Suffice to say that, after six or seven phone calls to the *Mairie* it was sorted out. Whilst all this was going on I was sitting outside on the grass, enjoying the sunshine and smoking (a sign says it's *'interdit'* in the office). I'd asked my interpreter her name (Martine), explained to her that I was English, not German and called MARSH (my first name was Peter), then asked her out for dinner. I'd made her giggle and I like that in a woman. Also, I was to have further use of her, but more of that later. I returned to the Café and ordered one (*'café au lait, s'il vous plait'*).

That morning, I'd moved Rip-Rap from the public car park to a spot near the *Club Nautique* and dis-assembled the rig. It was very strange driving the Volvo on her own again, she felt like a Grand Prix car. Despite huffing and puffing her way up a couple of dozen hills, boiling the brake fluid and having untold stress and strain put on her rear suspension parts, she seemed in remarkably fine fettle. I doubted if I would ever have to call upon the AA Five Star Service, but it was comforting to know it was there.

I told François about how ghastly the caravan was and he smiled. He'd told me it was small when he telephoned me to say he'd booked it and Rip-Rap's place on the pontoon, but I don't think he'd actually seen it, not inside anyway.

Then I handed out the presents, the whisky for François and Bruno ('Peetair, zis I know comes from zee 'eart'), a framed copy of Beth's panoramic pic of the lake with the shot of her sitting in front of 'Beth' cleverly superimposed and signed by Gaz, Beth and I under the inscription, 'To beautiful François and his beautiful family... a beautiful view'.

For the children, Sadie and Jules, *la pièce de résistance*, a signed copy of one of Beth's most popular books, recently published in French. They were thrilled and scampered to the back of the bar room to sit at the one and only table and read it. Katrine was most impressed and thanked me profusely. François kept holding up the picture all day and sighing. I think he likes it, he told me some days later that he'd put it on the wall in their bedroom.

Its just a pity Gaz hadn't made the trip with me as planned, but I somehow don't think it would have been quite the adventure if he had. On second thoughts, it could've been worse!

*

"Oo... Aargh!" Bruno exclaimed as he rolled painfully out of the Range Rover.

This was a good start to the day, I thought. We're supposed to be launching Rip-Rap and the prime mover for the whole operation has done his back in.

"You OK, Bruno?" I asked, stupidly.

It was bloody obvious that the man was in considerable pain.

"Allo everee... argh... bodee, aargh!" The claw shot out, touched my hand briefly, then dived into his trouser pocket once more. "Pas... aargh... de problème," he said, lighting up a Gitanes.

We hitched up the trailer to his Range Rover and I followed Rip-Rap along the promenade and down towards the slipway. It was a strange feeling following what had been following me all those hundreds of miles and I wondered how Bruno was going to handle this part of the operation. It's something I had worried about for some while.

Back in January, Gaz and I had measured the width of the slipway and tried to calculate the angle. There is a rusty old winch at the top of the slip, but no handle and it's probably solid anyway. Bruno reversed down onto the slip until the trailer wheels were in the water and indicated to François, who'd come along to help, that we should chock the trailer wheels with stones. This done, he disconnected the Range Rover and took it to the top of the slip. Then he told me to attach the safety strap, which held Rip-Rap onto the trailer, around his ball hitch and back to the trailer. It was all becoming blindingly obvious.

He took up the strain and François removed the stones as I climbed aboard. I'd rigged up the rudder, tiller and pansy electric motor whilst waiting for the boys to arrive so there was just the bow strap to remove and she was ready to go in. This done I went back to the cockpit and held my breath.

Bruno reversed slowly down, I couldn't see François but presumed he was steering the trailer with the jockey wheel. If he was he didn't do a very good job. The left hand trailer wheels slid off the edge of the slip and Rip-Rap and I were unceremoniously dumped into the lake. As we floated backwards I heard Bruno gun the Range Rover's engine and watched in horror as he yanked the trailer back onto the slip. The second launching of Rip-Rap I'd witnessed, both inauspicious.

It was a nerve-jangling moment watching one's possession being so roughly treated, but out the trailer came and remarkably little damage was done. I switched on the motor and took Rip-Rap round to the far side of the pontoon, tying on fenders and mooring lines as we went. The motor seemed to push Rip-Rap along OK and the Tillatenda held her straight. When I got there Bruno caught my mooring lines and handed the stern chain to me. I took it back and tied off. We were there. I lifted the cabin sole board just to check that there had been no ingress of water and we all left for the Café in order to take celebratory ale. Bruno said he would return at about three o'clock with another Bruno and we could step the mast, I was to prepare it.

It was to be a day of firsts — I'd never launched off a trailer before and never stepped a big boat's mast manually. I was in some dread as to how this was going to be carried out, especially with Bruno's bad back, but when I saw the size of the Bruno that Bruno had brought with him, the fear subsided. The man is enormous, ripples with muscles and despite giving one the initial impression that he's a complete drongo, turns out to be an absolute darling. He also said to me a while later, when the mast was up and rigged and copious *pastis* were being thrown around, that he thought Rip-Rap was the prettiest boat he'd ever seen, so Big Bruno can do no wrong in my eyes.

"I don't see the point of this letter. He is saying do it this way, but you can do it that. What is the point?"

"Now slow down a bit, old girl, tell me exactly what it says, word for word and very slowly."

I was showing my letter from M. Perrion of the CSRIN to Martine as I was determined to get an accurate explanation of the wording therein. Whilst François' English is passable for conversation, it's not so hot when it comes down to technicalities, like grammar. I'd shown the letter to him the day I arrived, he read it, smiled, handed it back to me with a shrug of the shoulders and said, 'Jus' do it'.

I still wasn't at all sure and I wasn't prepared to start putting posters up all over the place until I had proof positive that doing charters without registering my business activities was absolutely water tight in the legal department.

"It is this word here, *'soit'*. He starts this paragraph with *'soit'* and then this next paragraph with *'soit'*. You see?" Martine was explaining it beautifully.

"Right, but what in God's name does *'soit'* mean?"

"In this case, 'either, or'. You can either do it this way, or you can do it that."

"Right. And if I do it that," I pointed to the shorter paragraph, the one with the words *'pavillon de Grande Bretagne'* in it, "what precisely does it mean?"

"It means that you can do it under the British flag without registering your business in France."

Whoopee! At last, somebody had explained it to me, after all this time.

"OK. Next thing. My ICC is due to arrive at any time, then can we ring this man and ask him to confirm what he's said is correct? I have to be 100 per cent about this."

"Of course. He is in Marseille and I come from Marseille. He will know with my accent."

Brilliant. Things were taking a marked swing in the upwards direction.

A few days earlier, my fourth in Brouville, I'd gone to the *Mairie* and paid for a year on *le ponton*. It's actually cheaper than paying for four months, would you believe, but not advisable to leave your craft there over the winter however, and judging by the damage to the few boats which were tied to *le ponton* when we'd visited in January, I had absolutely no intention whatsoever of abandoning Rip-Rap to such a fate.

"Obviously honks a bit from time to time," Gaz had said, as we stared at one particularly sad sight.

So, with my dues paid to *la Commune de Brouville*, it was time for our first sail. I'd checked and double-checked all my rigging and spent some time T-Cutting the hull. The journey had left its mark, or rather, marks. A *camion* had sprayed the port side of the hull with some very sticky substance, the tree marks had to be removed and all the bouncing around she'd done had moved poor old Rip-Rap back a few inches causing nasty rubber marks to be transferred from the cradle to the hull. All those now removed, we were ready for the off.

It was a perfect breeze, 10 to 15 knots of wind and we headed for the northernmost point of the lake, where the waters from the Gorges du Durance finally arrive and deposit themselves in Le Lac. It was blowing from the south so we took a series of long broad reaches, gybing from one side of the lake to the other and two and a half hours later we entered the lagoon which heralds the entrance to the Gorges. Masses of water there, 25 metres on the echo sounder, but as I hadn't brought the dinghy, there was no point in stopping, so we turned to head back.

The return sail provided at least one interesting moment and gave me a warning of what was to come. The whole of the first part of the sail, from Brouville in the south right up to the entrance to the Gorges had been idyllic, the steady breeze was not the sort of wind you usually associate with inland waterways surrounded by mountains. I'd done a bit of dinghy racing on Lake Bala in North Wales and that environment is very similar. I'd expected the same twisty wind, funnelled as it is by the mountains, but Ste Serre seemed to be blessed by a steady breeze, more associated with sea yottin'.

On my return journey, beating against the still steady breeze I left my tacks as late as possible, going close to the shoreline and taking a peek at some of the lagoons, particularly on the west bank north of Sainte Serre village, which is mostly inaccessible by car and therefore would provide excellent venues for punters wishing to anchor up and party in some privacy. I was approaching one such lagoon and preparing to tack when suddenly hit by the most extraordinary gust — it came from above, the wind seemingly coming over the mountain ridge and hurtling down towards the surface of the lake.

Rip-Rap went over on her beam ends as I clung on to whatever

I could cling on to and rode the gust out. Round and round we went, like a funfair ride, seemingly for some minutes, as the wind continued to dump on us from above. It gradually eased and Rip-Rap righted herself, but I reefed in the jib just in case it happened again.

A few minutes later I was passed by another yacht going north and the helmsman was making circles with his forefinger, grinning hugely. I waved and smiled back, and made for the middle of the lake watching him as he approached the spot I'd been caught out in. The same thing happened, and I watched with some amusement as the yacht performed the same gyrations I had, just minutes before. It was spectacular to watch and gave rise to the title of this tome. I decided to give the lagoons up there a miss however and headed for the other side.

I tootled round the island off Les Gaps, echo sounder on and frequently referred to, as I knew from our January visit that the water level to which the lake lowers during the winter turns the island into an isthmus. I need not have feared, there was at least 12 metres at the shallowest point. That was in June, by early August the level would drop dramatically and it was only just possible to sneak around the island.

Les Gaps beach has nothing much to offer, there isn't even a beach bar, so I decided that I wouldn't visit there too often unless somebody wanted to go specifically. Sainte Serre beach is much the same, although there are one or two snack-bary sort of places. Also the beach itself slopes out very gently and it's necessary to anchor some way off and take the dinghy ashore. Other places it's possible to nose right up to the beach and step off the bows, in the entrance to the Gorges, for instance and in many of the lagoons which are dotted around the south and south west shoreline. Several long beats and three hours after leaving the Gorge, we tied up at *le ponton*. If I could do that each day of chartering it would make the perfect day out, giving the punters an hour or so to explore the Gorge in the dinghy or on a pedalo.

The next day was spent nearer to home exploring the southern shoreline of Le Lac. Despite not appearing on the Road Atlas of Europe, Le Lac de Ste Serre looms large on the Michelin road map of Provence and the southern end looked to have some interesting features. It did, although not the sort of features you usually find on road maps. Dotted along the shoreline, in sparse clusters were any number of nudists. All shapes and sizes were observed.

Now when enjoying our pub lunch on the day of departure, Mother had said to me,

"You do realise that you're fulfilling your father's lifelong ambition, don't you?".

I didn't, but right now I felt very, very close to Father. I was observing the shapes and sizes through his World War Two binoculars, previously utilised for observing the shapes and sizes of Messerschmitts, Dorniers, Heinkels and the like. Father had been in the Royal Artillery, anti-aircraft department. The nationality of my shapes and sizes were undoubtably the same as father's, you can tell by the colour of the hair, but I wasn't expecting my lot to drop anything on me.

I found the most amazing little lagoon tucked away at the southernmost end of the lake and nosed Rip-Rap into it, very, very slowly, keeping a constant eye on the echo sounder. A young couple were skinny-dipping as I entered the lagoon, but seemed completely at ease, the young man climbing to the top of a cliff and diving into the clear, greeny-blue water with everything dangling. There was 15 metres of water, so I dropped anchor and let out 20 of chain, then spent a delightful hour sipping beer and watching the young couple at play. For some reason I got the distinct impression that they were rather enjoying being watched and it wouldn't have surprised me if I'd got the full show. I didn't, you'll be relieved to hear, but I earmarked this place for another visit. Many other visits, as it turned out.

I'd used the motor quite a lot during my exploration of the coves, so I checked the voltmeter when I arrived back at the pontoon. It was down to 8 volts so I made the decision not to go out for a couple of days and let the Solar Battery Charger do its stuff. This was to prove a problem, the pansy electric motor used so much juice that the Solar Battery Charger needed a good week to re-charge it fully even from eight volts. WANCA Tony had been right in his observation that I would need a trickle charger, especially if I was to use the motor daily.

Whilst investigating the sail wardrobe when I first bought Rip-
Rap I'd discovered that she had a boom tent, but I'd only had it
up once, on a day of sheeting rain in Port Dinorwic. Being none
too sure how to rig it and the inclement weather being against my
doing the job properly, I'd not bothered with the thing since. Now
it was dug out as the Provence sun was in need of being blanked
out of the cockpit. I spent a while rigging it in a rough kind of way
and decided that it needed shock cord in order to do the job
properly. I knew there was a Surf-Centre at Les Gaps a few
kilometres away, so I paid it a visit in the Volvo.

Yes, the nice man did have shock cord, but he seemed loathe to
part with any. Eventually I persuaded him to let me have two 4
metre lengths at 8FF per metre and I returned to Brouville. Some
time was spent rigging the tent and it looks and works a treat,
giving me ample standing headroom in the middle, and
providing shelter from the worst of the midday sun. I quite often
used the cockpit for the purposes of writing this tale, it was a
relaxing and efficacious place in which to collect my thoughts and
impart them to you.

I was busy imparting my thoughts on the caravan and Le
Camping Municipal to François when Bruno happened along.
After the 'Allo everybodee'/handshake/fag-lighting routine had
been completed, Bruno listened to my tale of the hovel and
suggested that I pay a visit to Jean and Yvette who owned a
campsite just up the road from where I was at the Camping
Municipal. So I did. They seemed a delightful couple and 'yes'
they had a caravan available for August and September and
would I like to see it?

"I would," I said, and Yvette took me for a viewing, whilst Jean
jumped into his car and drove off.

It was no bigger than the one I was in but much newer and
smarter. It had electricity too, no gas or water though, but the
same price. All in all it seemed a better proposition as the
campsite had much better amenities and a Pizzeria. I said 'yes'

and drove back to my grim abode. On the way into Le Camping I was hailed by Martine who came out of reception to greet me.

"You are rich, Peetair," she said, and I wondered what she knew that I didn't. "You have electricity!"

The *Maire* it transpired had got drift of my rumblings and ordered a fifty metre cable to be purchased especially for my caravan. I was also informed that the facilities were now open for business and I inspected the shower and toilet block. It was fine and the showers had hot water. Now I was in a quandry — I'd just said 'yes' to Yvette and the *Maire* had done all this for me.

Also, Martine told me that she'd spoken to M. Perrion and a woman at the *Affaires Maritime* in Paris and everything was in order for me to charter under the British flag with the permission, in writing, of the *Maire*. Lordy, lordy, but politically I was in one hell of a spot. I decided to lay low on my decision to move campsites and went to the *Mairie* to make a *rendezvous*. All the Marsh tact and diplomacy was going to be required to sort this one out.

The lady at the *Mairie* said she would ring Le Camping when she'd spoken to the *Maire* and arranged a convenient time for me to see him, but I'd seen him before she'd had a chance. We bumped into each other that evening, as he headed for home and I headed for the Café.

Yes, he said, no problem, dug his diary out, thumbed through it and said *'Vendredi, à dix heure et demi'*. Smashing, tomorrow was *Vendredi*. I puzzled as to why he hadn't said *'à demain'* (tomorrow), but no matter, he's a fairly formal chap in all but his dress.

The next day dawned, once again brightly, and I prepared myself for the mayoral visit. I stopped by at the camping café, Le Cabanon as it is called, and ordered a coffee. Martine spotted me and came over holding a small piece of paper.

"It is a message for you, from the *Mairie*, about your meeting with the *Maire*."

"Yes, I know," I said, rather cockily. "I saw him last night and we made an appointment there and then. I'm on my way now."

"Pourquoi? The *rendezvous* is for tomorrow."

I took the note from her and pointed to the day.

JUST DO IT!

"Vendredi, Vendredi, today is *Vendredi."*

"No, today is *Jeudi.* Tomorrow is *Vendredi."*

Bollocks. I was starting to lose track of time. I'd have to start formalising myself a bit before I slid down the slippery slope and forgot that time existed at all. It wouldn't be long before time became nothing more than light bits and dark bits.

I returned to the caravan and dug out an exercise book which Beth had given to me on departure.

"I want you to keep notes daily," she had said. I had started to, but glancing at it now I realised that I hadn't filled it in for over a week and that's why time was slipping away.

I spent the rest of that light bit getting up to date and I was by the time the dark bit arrived.

"You see my friend, in Brouville zere is a light side and a dark side. Ze *Maire* and ze *Mairie,* myself, ze Café du Soleil, Bruno and *le Club Nautique* and now you and Rip-Rap, we are all on ze light side. Ze people of whom you speak, zey are on ze dark side."

I'd been telling François of an encounter I'd had with one Sylvan Arnoux, the chap who rents out the pedaloes from his cabin next to the pontoon. If all else failed, it had occurred to me that Sylvan could roll my chartering proposition into his business, after all renting out pedaloes was a damn sight nearer to what I was trying to do than running a café. Surely Sylvan would not have to register my activity with the authorities. I was wrong.

I'd been introduced to Sylvan by Harry, an Englishman of advanced years who had been coming to Brouville for twenty or more of them and at one time had owned a house here. When I'd first met Harry he was pottering with an old Enterprise dinghy he'd also once owned, but he'd now given it to Sylvan on the understanding that he could still go sailing in it. We'd had a long chat and he'd told me that he once used to be a member of *le Club Nautique* but had fallen out with the new younger people who'd come in and changed the way it was run. It had been, of course, a typical dinghy club run by a load of stuffed ones, but these stuffed ones were the likes of Harry, part-time Englishmen abroad, trying to impose their ways on the Gallic upstarts, one of whom was

97

Bruno, who, Harry rather scathingly informed me, wasn't French but Serbo-Croat.

Now this tale was beginning to sound mighty familiar, remember my ex-pal Richard and his attempts to change the ways of NYC and BYC? I'd been against that, in the UK it's better to go along with the stuffed ones, let them run the club and take your pleasures elsewhere, as the WANCAs had done. Now I was beginning to see exactly what it was Bruno had done. He'd taken the English stuffed ones by the scruff of the neck and given to Brouville not only a club which would provide a year-round facility for the youth of the village and surrounding district, but a registered branch of the national sailing school, the *Ecole Francais de Voile*. The club had been re-opened by one Eric Tabarly, whose sad and untimely death I had been informed of on the day of my arrival. It now has status and the likes of Harry have to accept it or do without it.

So here he was, in the public car park, fiddling and farting about with his ageing Enterprise and complaining that he couldn't use the workshop facilities of *le Club*. Then along came Sylvan, we were introduced and Harry told him of my plans and asked if there was any way he'd be prepared to co-operate. '*Non*', was the simple answer, but he launched into the boring ritual of telling me everything I'd have to do, all of which of course I knew already, and he finished up with the threatening comment that, 'Brouville was a small place and everybody knew everybody else's business and *les flics* came around quite frequently to check on authorisation and such.' Nice bloke, Sylvan, and as he was ideally positioned to keep an eye on my activities, some 20 metres from Rip-Rap at the end of the pontoon, I had better tread warily.

François, after explaining about the dark and light sides of Brouville, also told me a sweet tale about the threatening Sylvan's father. Transpires he was once the charismatic but autocratic *Maire* of Brouville, who curried favour with the likes of the ageing English stuffed ones. Their habit of buying holiday homes in *la Commune* was bumping up property values to some tune. Amongst many political misdoings he'd tried to get the Café du Soleil closed down, in a very underhand way and also spent the

Commune's money willy-nilly. The light side rose.

Maire Duchatel, my pal, was elected in place of the Maire of Darkness, Arnoux, but not before the Dark One had managed to get son Sylvan elevated to Head Firebobby however, and that along with his proper profession of plumber, renting out the pedaloes, flogging ice creams from his shack and having a boat repairing business. Rules are made to be broken, as we were rapidly finding out. No wonder young Sylvan didn't want to run the risk of a close scrutiny by *les flics* if they came round checking things out. Couldn't hide behind daddy any more, could he?

Some time during that day's dark bit I was surrounded by my new friends from the light side and *le Président* Bruno said,

"Sylvan Arnoux, *il est* one to talk!".

We were in the Café, chuntering of this and my chartering situation. The light side raised their glasses and said, almost in unison,

"Jus' do it!"

I doffed my Nike hat to them, looked at the logo and wondered if for once fate had at last stumbled in and landed on my side. I raised my glass and shouted,

"Just do it!"

Chapter 7

MR GOODBODY'S WALL

*In which I tell of my daily routine, a visit from
my oldest friend Dave and some tales of
Regattas past and present.*

As mentioned, time and the keeping of it was becoming a problem.

First thing in the morning was instantly recognisable; it was when I woke up. Thereafter, I'd developed some sort of schedule, a daily format which was more or less kept to, most days anyway. This was necessary for my sanity. I'd realised when mistaking *Jeudi* for *Vendredi* that I was in danger of turning my whole life into one long mong and that simply wouldn't do. The whole trip to Provence had been intended, not only for me to try and earn a daily crust doing the charters, but to write this tome.

The story had really started back in September and I'd written the first couple of chapters then, but I'd realised that what I had written had no mileage as a short story or magazine article — the tale had to be developed and I was the only one who could develop it. If you've reached this point, dear reader, you will know by now that quite a lot of developing had gone on. But I still wasn't writing and that worried me, so I set about making my notes in Beth's exercise book longer and more detailed. That was most part of the morning sorted out in my new daily schedule. Thence to the Café for late morning coffee and a breakfast of *croissant* and marmalade. Then to the boat, for a period of fettling. There are always things to fettle on a boat, one such thing was a curious browny stain in the cockpit, cleaned up daily yet still there the next day. It was a mystery which took many weeks to solve.

One item that needed a major dose of looking at was the drop centreboard which wouldn't — drop that is. It is operated by two stainless steel cables which are connected to a looped rope on pulleys. I'd had this problem the previous year and no amount of heaving on the ropes would budge it, not even putting the 'down' rope onto one of the primary winches. All that did was burn a groove in the coachroof. I had ended up putting Rip-Rap in the travel hoist at Dinas yard in Port Dinorwic, to enable Duncan and I to lever the thing out, which with some difficulty we eventually did. It stayed down all season and I just had to come to terms with having a five-foot draught instead of a three-foot one.

When I pulled Rip-Rap out in October I'd spent some time making sure the centreboard was free and it certainly seemed to be before being tucked up for the winter on the trailer. Now the old problem had returned. When Dunc and I had got the thing out, it was the first few inches that were the hardest. Once it was about six inches down the thing just fell out, so I tied Rip-Rap side on to the pontoon, close to the shore, donned a diving mask and went into the water with a long-handled screwdriver, the same implement we'd used successfully the previous year, but I kept on running out of breath before making too much progress. Harry sauntered down the pontoon and announced that he was going for a swim. He asked what I was doing and I told him. He volunteered to have a go, with similar results. The bloody thing was stuck up its slot and destined to stay there. I put on some dry clothes and put the boat back on her mooring.

Each non-yottin' day, at about four o'clock I'd repair once more to the Café and partake of ale, usually a pint of *panaché*, shandy to the English. It was ice cold and thirst-quenching, as well as being bloody expensive. I don't know why the ale lobbyists in England bang on about the price of English beer compared to that of the Eurofizz served in French bars. This simple pint of *panaché* was setting me back £2.50 and despite the fact that it was served in a genuine Kronenbourg pint pot, I never actually got a whole pint because there was always a good two inches of froth on top. This *panaché* hour was also a good time to chew the cud with François before he went off for his siesta. I'd later return to the campsite for an early evening noggin, after showering and changing.

Telephone watch at the Café took place between 8 and 9 o'clock French time. I'd told everybody in England that I would be there between 7 and 8 BST, so I was. And that gives rise to another imponderable; why can't everywhere in the world be the same time? It'd make life a lot easier and does it really matter what exact hour folk go to work, or milk the cows, or go to the pub, or wake up? "I got up at three o'clock" wouldn't sound too enthusiastic or alternatively too decadent, would it? It would simply be a statement of fact. Round-the-world yachtsmen rely on GMT, (four hours on — four hours off), so why not the other 99.9 recurring percent of us? This system would also cure jet-lag, so all the posy, high-flying executives would have no excuse to take an extra golf-playing day or two off after their recurring golf-infested trips to America or the Far East.

There is only one place in the world where time doesn't exist, the International Date Line. It is an invisible and imaginary line drawn from pole to pole and roughly on the other side of the globe from the Greenwich Line. It runs down the middle of the Pacific, squiggling here and there to avoid any land mass, even the tiniest of islands. And that's where Gaz and I plan to see the next millennium in, sitting in his boat, slap bang on the International Date Line. So 31st December 1999 and 1st January 2000 for us two WANCAs at least, will not exist, or at least merge into one. Should be fairly quiet too and it'll only take 24 hours to pack in two days' excitement.

Telephone watch became my *pastis* hour, usually shared with a Bruno or two and which ended when Mr Goodbody's wall turned pink. The setting sun on the other side of the lake caused this phenomenon, not the *pastis*, and you could set your watch by it, 9 o'clock, on the dot.

Mr Goodbody I had met in September and I've introduced you to him in Chapter Two. Sadly he wasn't around at this time, the Provence summers being too hot for him. He now only stays in Brouville from September to May. Thankfully his wall was still there, and its change of hue served to remind me that it was time to eat and switch to red wine. Milko knew my routine, he very quickly sussed it and my drink of the hour was always delivered to my table without a word being exchanged. He also knew what

I ate — *'Entrecôte aux Herbes avec pommes frites, pour l'Anglais'*, that means 'well-done' in English restaurant parlance.

It was a Friday afternoon, the afternoon after the morning in which I'd had my meeting with the *Maire* and I was having my cud-chewing *panaché* hour with François. We'd talked for a few minutes, I'd told him that my meeting had gone well, that the *Maire* understood I could charter with his permission, sailing under the British flag and he would write me a letter of authority to that effect. François had just said 'I told you so' when customers hoved into view and he left me in order to give them attention, it being Milko's time off. I sat on the terrace, sipping my shandy and gazing idly over the lake. The Mistral was blowing and the surface of the water was quite choppy. Suddenly, out of the corner of my eye, I saw the Enterprise with Harry in it shoot out from behind the slipway, whiz across the lake and disappear behind the trees on a headland the other side of the lagoon. This was all a bit surprising, as Harry had told me during the morning that he was having problems with his centreboard which was the opposite to mine — his was stuck down and, if you're going to go whizzing as close to shore as Harry was now, you'd need to have your centreboard operational.

It was five minutes before Harry re-appeared, on his own, *sans* boat. He was standing on the headland shore, waving his arms wildly about and moments later I saw his wife paddling across in their two-man canoe. All most confusing. She landed on the headland and they both disappeared into the trees, to re-appear minutes later dragging the Enterprise. At last I realised what had happened, as they tied the dinghy painter onto the canoe and paddled off towing it. Harry had not disappeared behind the headland, he'd disappeared into it, presumably totally out of control in the strong and gusty wind. Well, I thought, that'll have cured his sticking centreboard problem!

François returned from serving his customers and I started to tell him a little bit about my oldest friend Dave. I say oldest, we are the same age to within a month, what I really mean is I've know Dave longer than anyone outside my family, and longer than most of them.

My earliest recollection of this radical left-wing scoundrel is that of my fourth birthday party. He'd climb a door, an awesome feat for a four year old, and sit on top of it berating all and sundry beneath him until removed from said perch by an adult. Undeterred he'd do it again, a different door though. I guess his theory was that the adults would be confused and not know where he was going to pop up next. Always did like his soapbox, our Dave, and after leaving university he joined the Mirror Group of newspapers, finally ending up as deputy editor of the Mirror itself. This elevated position he vacated of his own accord last autumn, it was all quite voluntary, no adult was there to lift him down although the scandalous Mr Maxwell had had a serious attempt to lift Dave and several thousand others down some years previously. I mention Dave because that Friday afternoon whilst talking about him to François, I had the strangest feeling he was going to turn up.

David and I had partaken of a dry sherry or two at his parents' house around the festive season and he'd told me of his plan to buy a campervan and drive around Europe gathering material for a book he planned to write. I'd told him of *La Bonne Idée* and he said he'd try to include me in his schedule.

Not five minutes after François had retired for his siesta and I was settling my bar bill with Milko in the Café, the unmistakable profile of one David Charles Lamb passed the doorway in a white campervan. I shot out of the door but it was too late — Dave was through the village square and off out the other side. He had spotted the Café du Soleil, however, and returned on foot having found a temporary resting place for Daisy, his trusty steed. I was in for a good weekend and a huge dollop of motivation.

Dave has always had an acerbic turn of wit and this has presumably helped him through his chosen occupation of the past thirty two years, writing tabloid headlines. We were genuinely enjoying each other's company, albeit in strange surroundings, and whilst joining me in the early evening noggin at the campsite where he'd parked Daisy next to my caravan, he told of his adventures of the past five weeks.

The German tourists in particular, outnumbering all other nationalities put together in some of the places Dave had visited, were on the receiving end of the Lamb wit with lines like 'obscene vowel movements' and 'umlautish behaviour' being written in the copious notes he was making. Well, they weren't really notes, he was practically writing the book as he went, spending the first five hours of most days sitting at a makeshift desk in Daisy and filling a school library full of exercise books with his ramblings. I showed him the lap-top I'd brought with me and he was mightily impressed, saying that it was just the sort of thing he could do with. He was going to return to England and re-write his story on his computer, an awesome task that I felt he wasn't relishing the thought of. I was somewhat sheepish when he asked how I was getting on and I replied that I hadn't even switched the thing on yet.

"Get on with it for Christ's sake. Your whole life'll slip by before you've written a single sodding word!"

That was just the rocket I needed and the day we hugged and said our goodbyes, I took out the lap-top and started. Thanks Dave.

I cannot leave the honourable Lamb there however, you have a need to learn more of our weekend together, dearest one. The first night, the noggins being finished, we journeyed to the Café for my telephone watch. Dave had outlined his thoughts on the evening: a few *pastis*, a good meal, if possible discover the result of, or better still, watch the England v. Columbia match and early to bed. He'd driven over the Alps that day and was a bit on the knackered side. It dove-tailed exactly with what I had in mind, all that is except the football, but for Dave I would make an exception. The *pastis* were delivered to our table by a wordless Milko and Dave and I nattered the hour away. Beth rang however, and that made my vigil worth while. I was pleased not to have broken my usual daily schedule for the second time that day. Mr Goodbody's wall turned pink and I indicated to Milko that his attention was required. He stepped efficiently up and before I had a chance to utter a word, he said,

"Deux, pour les Anglais? Et un litre de rouge?"
I said 'yes', introduced Dave to Milko and explained what it was
we'd just ordered. Dave was amused and went along with the
order. François also came over and he too was introduced, but he
changed the order to roast veal. He obviously had a surplus and
had found a good way of getting rid of it.

Dave was mightily taken with the antics of these two. In the
time I'd been there I'd got used to the double act of Milko running
the bar and waiting side, whilst François did his thing in the
kitchen, throwing lumps of meat and pasta about. It was all new
to Dave however, and the sight of Milko standing on one leg,
shading his eyes and scanning the street this way and that in a
vain attempt to locate potential customers had Dave in fits. Milko
reminded him of a young Jacques Tati, an all-time favourite of
both of us, and I had to agree that there was a resemblance.

On the day after I had arrived in Brouville, François was briefing
his summer team and decided that he needed a trigger word to
shout from the kitchen, an unmistakable one indicating that a
meal had been prepared and was ready for delivery. As I had said
I was on my holidays and this had obviously stuck in François'
mind, the shout of 'Oliday!' had become familiar to all of us, all
that is except Dave. With all the antics going on, Milko's
pantomime act and waiters and waitresses scurrying to the
kitchen door every time François bellowed 'Oliday!', Dave found
the whole farce very amusing and said he was going to include it
in his book. We enjoyed the veal, although it was a bit on the
stringy side. When I told Beth this on the phone a day or two later
she suggested that we might have been served donkey. Nothing
would surprise me.

England beat Columbia and we managed to watch the second
half on Le Cab's TV, so Dave went to bed a happy man that night
as indeed did I. It was great to share my new yet temporary life
with someone so good to be with.

The following day I left Dave doing his scribbling and went to
prepare Rip-Rap for an afternoon's yott. When she was collecting
the camping dues the previous evening I'd introduced Martine to
Dave. 'The third Mrs Marsh?', he'd ventured, after she'd left. It's

a joke he'd started the first time I'd introduced him to a female companion after my second divorce, and I guess it'll continue until I marry again and after.

We'd all agreed that an afternoon's yottin' was in order as Martine had from one o'clock until five off. She'd been sailing with me once before and seemed to thoroughly enjoy it. Rip-Rap needs quite a bit of preparing for a sail, the boom tent has to be de-rigged, sail cover taken off, motor screwed on, padlocks removed, a general tidy up and the Hostess put away. That done, I motored over to the campsite beach, threw the hook down and awaited the arrival of my guests. They were late, but the time passed quickly enough — there was more Germanic nudity to be observed on the southern shore.

We set off and Martine asked if there was enough time to take a trip around the only island on the lake, in the bay off Les Gaps. She used to go there with her ex-husband, she explained and the eyebrows on Dave's heavily sun-blocked face shot up. 'The third Mrs...' was all he managed to get out before I hit him. He'll get me into serious bother one of these days.

It was, however, a most pleasant sail, the log suddenly decided to work after a long period of inactivity and the others took great glee in spotting our fastest speed. Dave was also fascinated with the echo sounder, we achieved a record 84 metres that afternoon. Declaring that she was too hot, Martine climbed into the dinghy being towed behind, threw herself into the water and hung off the back of the dinghy. I was amazed how it stopped Rip-Rap absolutely dead, but then Martine let go as a gust came and filled the sails once more. I turned and picked her up.

For most of last season I'd been on the end of some mickey-taking about my swimming ladder, affixed to Rip-Rap's transom at the time of purchase. I was rather pleased with it and doubted the gibbers when they said it'd never be used for its real purpose. The top half of it was used of course for getting onto the boat from the dinghy, but until now the bottom half had stayed firmly folded up as not a lot of swimming had been done in the chilly Irish Sea. It came in damn useful that afternoon when Martine made her dripping way up it and back into the cockpit.

The day was tinged with a sad moment however, when Martine lost the sun-hat which had been given to her by her grandmother thirty years previously. It blew off and sank without trace. It was a rather sad little person that we dropped off at the campsite beach, then Dave and I took Rip-Rap back to the pontoon.

"Where the hell is it?" I muttered to myself, my eyes scanning the water for the fender I left tied to the stern chain.

When going out single-handed this makes for an easy pick-up when approaching the pontoon and is a development of the idea suggested to me by the Lifeboat Coxwain when leaving my anchor chain in Moelfre Bay. I could lean over the side of the cockpit and pick it up with the boathook, stopping Rip-Rap dead before she hit the pontoon. I'd given the boathook to Dave and instructed him on what to do, but there was no sign of the fender. Then I spotted it.

Whilst we were making our sedate way around the Les Gaps island, we'd been passed at great speed by a large RIB, powered it seemed, by a mighty big outboard, and a petrol one at that. 'Sapeurs Pompiers', Martine had said. The Firebobbies. One rule for us, another for them. They hadn't been going to a fire, simply exerting their macho authority on the poor yotties struggling to find which way the wind was blowing and how best to harness it, for the pansy little electric devices we are forced to use are worse than useless for anything other than propelling ourselves off and on to the pontoon. And no doubt they thought they were impressing assorted topless tottie on Les Gaps beach.

The Sapeurs Pompiers will enter this tale once more, so I'll not dwell too long on what happened next. My fender was tied onto the transom of the Firebobbies inflatable, which was in turn padlocked to my mooring chain, the one I'd paid 1500FF to the Mairie for one year's use of. I was bloody seething. It was obviously a private mooring and the Head Firebobby, one Sylvan Arnoux, knew it. I looked scathingly at the group of Pompiers gathered outside their garage as we turned side on to the pontoon and I jumped ashore to hold the mooring lines. They glared arrogantly back, but nobody made a move. It was going to be bloodshed if I went to them, probably mine, so I asked Dave if he would have a diplomatic word. He speaks very passable French does Dave, and he can be diplomacy itself when the occasion arises. He did, and eventually the surliest *Pompier* of all sauntered casually down the pontoon, flicked his fag carelessly into the hallowed waters and made a fifteen minute meal of unlocking the smelly inflatable, throwing my fender into the neighbouring yacht.

Such was the volume of steam coming out of my ears, as without a word I retrieved my fender and made a lock job on Rip-Rap that Houdini himself would have died' trying to get out of, it was a very relieved Dave who took me by the arm and led me silently away from the pontoon and in the general direction of the nearest bar. I gathered that the eye contact I had with young Arnoux as we passed the surly group gave him the impression that I was just a little annoyed however, as his attitude towards me after that was in the main very pleasant and the smelly inflatable was kept on the other side of the pontoon.

Several beers were had and thence to the Café du Soleil for the *pastis* hour and telephone watch. Dave offered to pay for the meal, the agreement I'd told him I had to have with any punters, until I had received my written authority from the *Maire*. It was a lovely and very generous gesture which I appreciated then and still do. I felt as if I'd had my first customer and a better one I couldn't imagine.

Mr Goodbody's wall turned pink and *'Deux, pour les Anglais'* were ordered. This time we got them, delicious *entrecôte* steaks, not a stringy donkey in sight. The two Brunos turned up and invited me to join in a *'Regatte'* which was due to start at 10.30 the following morning. I tried to persuade Dave to stay an extra day and crew for me, but no, the Freddie Mercury tape was cued up in Daisy's stereo and he was off to Barcelona to start his tour of Spain and Portugal.

When we hugged goodbye the next morning and I thought that we must be turning truly European, we promised to let each other know how things turned out. He'd given me the kick-start I needed, and for that I'm truly grateful.

*

I'm not fiercely competitive, but racing does give you a purpose to yott, some place to aim for and get to. The *Regatte* which I'd been persuaded to join by the two Brunos didn't really happen. I'd gone to the Club pontoon single-handed at the appointed time, 10.30, and hovered around whilst four or five other boats came round from the Municipal pontoon. They tied up to the Club pontoon and went ashore then came back to their boats and set off. I followed, but there were no sound or flag signals, no marker buoys or a shore transit to denote the start line, they just set off.

By the fourth tack I was ahead of them and had to hold back in order to discover where we were all going. They seemed to be heading for Ste Serre village so I guessed there must be some kind of a mark there, but no, just the usual few boats riding on their moorings. By this time all the other boats had scattered to the four corners of the lake so I gave up and headed off for the north end, threw down the hook and had a picnic.

Later that evening, sipping *pastis* in the Café, I collared one of the Brunos and asked about the *Regatte*. It was Big Bruno who's Provençal accent I don't understand too well, especially when he's been on the aniseed-flavoured rocket fuel all day, so I didn't get much sense out of him.

There had been a *Regatte*, of that there was no doubt, he kept on repeating it,

"*Regatte, oui. Regatte,* good."

One of the more memorable *Regattes* I've ever been involved in was at Pwllheli four or five years before. I'd done Dinghy Week with Luke and my mother had come down for a day out and to take him home whilst I stayed on to help with some restoration work on a pal's yacht, a 70 foot iron ketch which had been built in Hamburg just after the war. I could write a book about the adventures I've had on Black Knight and may well do so one day, so I won't bore you with too much now. Suffice to say that that was where I was and, during a beer-soaked evening with my pals in the Yacht Club, I got chatting to a chap who owned an ageing Carter 44, a yacht which in truth was really well past its racing days, but was there to take part in Celtic Race Week. He invited me to join them on the following day's race, so I did.

There was serious opposition, largely from a fleet of Sigma 38's who had come down from the Clyde, and the crew I was to sail with spent some while taking the mickey out of the Scots. The boys from north of the border didn't take too kindly to all this, although I found it hilarious. The start next morning was delayed due to lack of wind and the boats just milled around waiting for something to happen. The constant gibbing of our crew towards the Caledonians continued with comments like,

"You've time to go back to Pwllheli and get properly coiffed up!"

Then the buckets came out.

It all started very quickly, one boat motoring up alongside a competitor on the pretext of wanting to find out something or another and then the crew of the other boat got a drenching. It was mayhem for the next half hour, no boat in the fleet was spared, especially ours. The Scots ganged up on us and we were completely wet through when suddenly the wind got up and we were all called to the line.

We got a storming start, the helmsman was an ace. At the first mark he dived under three other boats and forced them to tack away. After that we had it in the bag. We were leading on the water and eventually finished third. That evening at the prizegiving, handicaps having been worked out, we'd won by just over a second. Close, or what?

A celebration was in order and dutifully carried out by the owner, who was still smiling when I saw him at the Boat Show five months later. My fellow crew members had a ball with the Scots, a memorable night indeed.

As the summer wore on and the days shortened the exact time at which Mr Goodbody's wall turned pink moved forward, almost imperceptibly at first, but by mid-August it was happening around 8.30. It became positively psychedelic as we were treated to one spectacular sunset after another. Each night I took my camera to the Café and took a snap or two. Then I realised how silly I was and that all I'd have to show folk was a spectacular sky. They are worth seeing though, the sunsets, not my snaps.

The more vivid and dramatic the clouds at this time the more vivid and dramatic would be the thunder and lightning which followed. Positively tropical. Generally speaking the storms passed quickly and we soon returned to the customary bright blue sky and brilliant sunshine. I had worried about how I'd take the heat, we had 42 degrees Celsius one day. After a while it became oppressive, especially around mid-afternoon in late July, so I took to the shade on the days I wasn't yottin'. I simply had to stay out of the direct sun to stop from frazzling up.

When yottin', I learnt to point Rip-Rap in certain directions so that I could sit in the shade of the sail. It didn't really matter which way I was going just as long as I was sailing and sitting in the shade, the big advantage of lake yottin', no course to stick with. Ultimately though, boring, despite the wonderful weather and the fact that I could just go for a yott at the drop of a hat.

When Mr Goodbody returned to Brouville for his winter sabbatical, the time at which it became necessary for my return to England's shores, I realised that that was something I should miss more than anything. Spontaneous yottin'.

Chapter 8

MACHO MEN, AND MACHO TWATS AND DOGS

*In which you will learn of my observations of
the French macho ones, male and female,
various dog incidents and the Sapeurs
Pompiers, part-time Pumped Up Soppy Ones.*

To me, pond fishing is a pastime of pansies. I cannot for the life
of me find one single macho thing about the sport, if sport it
is. The poor defenceless scaly things stand absolutely no chance
whatsoever as a barrage of hooks with coloured little wriggly
things on are thrown in their direction by assorted tanned, gum-
chewing, tattooed and mostly flabby men wearing cut-down T-
shirts.

The fish are trying to eat, for heaven's sake. It's a very natural
thing to do, and they spend a very large part of their light bits
and, for all I know, dark bits as well, simply trying to stay alive by
eating. To discover that, what they thought was a mid-morning
snack, lunch or afternoon tea is in fact a gruesome way of bringing
about their untimely death, must come as something of a shock. It
must be bad enough to discover that the tempting little morsel has
a bloody great spike skewered through it and that spike is now
stuck firmly in your mouth as you are dragged towards the shore
at twice the speed of sound. Imagine then what it must feel like
when you reach aforementioned shore and the spike is ripped out
of your mouth before your misery is terminated by having your
head bashed against a rock half a dozen times.

Ah, I see now — that's the macho bit, braining a poor
defenceless fish the size of your little finger. And are they taken
home to eat? No. They spend the rest of the day in a bucket and
then they're chucked back in the water. What is the point of all
this? I have pondered on it many times, all to no avail.

I suppose these rod-danglers, I can't bring myself to call them fishermen, probably feel the same way about us yotties, judging by the amount of abuse hurled at me one day as I left for a pleasant afternoon's yottin'.

The pontoon to which Rip-Rap was attached for most of the time is as a magnet for rod-danglers. They flock to it in droves from a very early hour in the day, the light bit just beginning. Then they spread their tackle about, attach wriggly things to hooks and spend the day staring steadfastly at colourful little floaty things. The assault course which the yotties have to negotiate in order to reach their vessels makes the Krypton Factor look easy. Why in God's name they feel a need to go to the pontoon I know not, the lake has twenty odd miles of accessible shoreline, quite a few of those miles littered with assorted nudists. Wouldn't that be a more favourable venue for the macho pansies? Apparently not. Perhaps they're frightened of getting their hooks caught in something as they cast the floaty thing, hook and worm out into the greeny-blue waters.

Leaving the pontoon in a yacht therefore is mighty hazardous, always assuming that you have got to the vessel unscathed. I had struggled manfully over the assault course, de-rigged the boom tent and cover and screwed the motor on before casting off and making my way gingerly in reverse. That was when the abuse started.

I looked around but could find no one other than myself who could have been the target of this invective. I looked towards the disappearing pontoon and pointed at my chest. The points which were returned were directed at Rip-Rap's waterline, somewhere around the stern. I looked over the transom and spotted what was clearly the item to which the macho pansies were directing my attention — a fishing line with a colourful floaty thing and a fish attached to it was caught around the prop.

I switched the motor off, pulled the engine up out of the water and started to unravel the string. It broke and the fish made its bid for freedom with the hook still in its mouth and trailing the floaty thing. I was reminded of Jaws.

On completion of the unravelling I turned to the pontoon and shrugged my shoulders, holding my hands wide apart. I cannot understand any colloquial French so I hadn't a clue what they were saying, but I could guess. The motor went back on and I left, hoping that they'd have had their fill of rod-dangling by the time I returned.

I was able to observe quite a lot of the life of a macho pansy whilst using the cockpit of Rip-Rap as an office.

The other accessory they all seem to have, apart from all the tackle which is spread around them, is a dog. Now one thing I have observed about the French macho man for a good many years is his dog.

It is his dog. It is not his wife's dog, it is not the family's dog, it is his dog. He is compelled to have this dog as a release, because he has a wife and a family. Therefore he is no longer the boss, no longer in charge and that hurts him. It is, of course, his macho pride which has been hurt, not him personally and so, in order to restore the status quo, macho man will spend hours catching fish and berating this other poor defenceless creature with an endless stream of invective.

I say 'poor' and 'defenceless' because that is what it is. The macho pansy will not have a Doberman, or a Rottweiller, or an Alsatian, these are owned by the single French females, presumably as some sort of defence against the attentions of the macho ones. No, he will have a tastefully clipped poodle, or a little fluffy terrier type of thing with ribbons in its hair, but always male for some reason. Perhaps the monthly doings of women are something to do with all this.

So macho man will have a male dog, a pal, but something he can hurl abuse at whilst thinking of the wife or one of his kids who is being unruly and won't do as it's told.

The invective usually if not always starts very suddenly and without warning and it is always just invective. You will never see a macho one hit his dog, he's too frightened of possible retaliation. They can carry a fearsome nip some of these pretty little things. No, it's abuse only, because a dog cannot answer back, not in French at least, and if it does venture a bark, a hand is raised. The little thing then scampers away knowing what's coming because he's seen his master give the kids a belt or two and that must hurt because they cry. The invective stops, just as suddenly as it started.

I was watching one such performance whilst idly brewing a coffee one morning. The abuse had finished after the hand-raising brought it to a close, the dog scampered away and the macho pansy returned his attentions to his colourful floaty thing. I went down to the cabin and did the necessary with the kettle, which had boiled up as the rod-dangler's temper simmered down.

Upon my return to the cockpit, I observed the clipped, but scruffy poodle playing with something in its mouth and being dive-bombed by two birds who daily strutted the pontoon. I couldn't work out what was going on and the macho one just continued to stare at the water, so I thought no more about it, rolled a fag and started to sip my coffee.

It was five minutes later when I was brought out of my reverie by shouts from the embryonic macho pansy, son of the big one. It was the bird's nest that the poodle had been playing with, cleverly concealed it would seem in the structure of the pontoon, the birds presumably having built it during the winter when rod-danglers don't operate. It must have seemed an idyllic setting for a home back in January. I'd thought so.

The damned pooch had torn the nest to shreds and munched the two chicks therein to death. They floated by uncaring, expectant mouths open for the last time as the macho pansy patted his poodle and congratulated the pooch on a job well done.

I'm not a huge fan of dogs, with one or two exceptions, but I particularly loathe the type of dog favoured by the French macho ones. It therefore came as something of a surprise to myself one day when leaving the pontoon for a spot of yottin', that I became involved in a noble piece of good-deedery.

My attention was drawn by a rod-dangler who was waving and shouting at me.

"*Chien! Chien!*" he was shouting and pointed at the water in front of Rip-Rap.

Eyes squinting against the bright sunlight reflecting off the water, I spotted a dog's head in the lagoon, a pink ribbon tied tastefully in its hair. I motored towards the head which was heading rapidly towards the far bank of the lagoon and broke out a mooring line. Putting the motor onto its lowest setting as I approached the head, I clamped the Tillatenda, went to the bows and lassooed it — initially. My lassoo slipped, or the dog did. The rope ended up around its right rear leg.

Unceremoniously, the pooch was hauled out of the water and onto the deck.

Tying off the mooring line to ensure that the dripping wet thing stayed on the foredeck, I ripped the ribbon out of its hair for devilment and chucked it overboard. Then I returned to the pontoon, the macho one catching the pulpit as I came up alongside. Untying the pooch I smugly handed the chap his beloved, this had to be worth a pint, surely, but it wasn't his. He just took the wet thing from me, put it down on the pontoon, shrugged at me and wandered back to his rod, which was dangling on its own.

'Macho twat', I thought, pushing off and putting once more to sea. God I hate them.

Martine also, it transpires, is not a great fan of the macho ones either.

"All they want to do is drink, smoke, swear and fuck," she imparted to Dave and I on our afternoon's sail.

"Sounds all right to me," Dave had ventured, but I know his tongue was firmly in the side of his mouth.

Poor old Martine, not only did she lose her beloved sun hat that afternoon, she told us that her boyfriend had ditched her, on the telephone the night before.

"On the bloody telephone, I ask you. What is that, insensitive or what?" she seethed, like a macho woman scorned.

"Maybe, but a very safe place to do it from, don't you think?" Dave was very amused with Martine's company and couldn't stop taking the mickey. When you get to know him it's great fun listening to his quick wit and repartee, but Martine had difficulty understanding it and was clearly annoyed.

117

"Listen, all the men in my life have been right on the edge, you know what this is? Right in between sanity and insanity, sometimes this way, sometimes that."

"Sounds like all the men in my life too," came the expected reply.

"No, you don't understand. Maybe I drive them mad, I don't know. Maybe they're mad already and just don't show it, until I get to know them." She paused, momentarily. "Perhaps I shall find a woman."

"Now that sounds more like it!" exclaimed Dave.

"Can we watch?" I ventured.

"You're all the fuckin' same, you macho men!"

Oops. Perhaps this was not a good time to try the English repartee on a poor defenceless and ditched little French creature.

"OK," I said. "Tell you what, Martine, I'll help you find one, how's that?"

I wasn't really joking either, it would be a mighty good challenge, but I didn't think Brouville was quite the right place to look. I was wrong.

"Can we go out for a meal, or just a drink or something? This place is driving me mad."

It was four or five days since Dave had left and I hadn't seen much of Martine since. My writing had started and I was keeping a fairly low profile on my re-structured daily routine. Morning coffee was taken at Le Cabanon, with *croissant* and marmalade, and I then returned to the caravan or more usually went to the boat to write. That was the whole day taken up, until around six in the evening when I wandered up to the Café to confuse Milko by ordering a beer in the no-man's land between *panaché* and *pastis* time. Then back to the caravan to shower and change before returning to do the telephone watch.

That much at least hadn't changed, but I'd decided to eat at the Café less often, preferring instead to snack my way through the day with a couple of *baguettes*, ham, cheese or *pâté*, and a beef tomato or two. The turning pink of Mr Goodbody's wall signalled time to go and read through what I'd written during the day and make notes about the next day's scribblings. One very infuriating night, probably too tired to concentrate, I made a mistake on a file name in the lap-top's memory and wiped out two days' work. I changed this reading hour to the mornings and read a book at night instead. I'd found a source for the locally produced red wine at 11.50FF a litre, very drinkable and an ideal nightcap — or daycap. I was sipping a glass of this stuff when Martine made her request.

"Yes. Don't see why not. I've got to go to the Café to do my telephone watch, so why don't you join me."

Martine said she would and scampered off to change. Half an hour later we were sitting outside the Café, a *pastis* for me and a *pamplemousse* for Martine, when a most curious sight hoved into view.

Mid-length hair, tinged red (or is it titian?) and parted in the middle, a tanned, square-jawed head with a craggy face, the mouth of which had gold-capped teeth which chewed gum. All this atop the thick-set and muscular neck which jutted out of proud, square shoulders. A large tattoo covering the more than adequate left bicep depicted a fire-spitting dragon.

My eyes moved down, past the loose-fitting, cut-away running shirt to the incredibly well formed legs, legs that were obviously used to running the odd marathon or two before breakfast. The trainers were a dead give-away, at least a hundred quids' worth, the professional sort, and jogging along beside the trainers was a neatly-clipped poodle with a ribbon in its hair, a male poodle at that.

Six foot of macho man personified.

My gaze went back up the legs to where the ample thighs were encased in purple Lycra and my eyes shot out of their sockets. This was no macho man, the Lycra was seriously deficient in the Linford Christie department. A genuine 100% macho twat!

"Don't look now Martine, but I think I've found her."

"Found who?"

"Your ideal partner."

Martine couldn't resist it. She turned to take in the apparition, then turned back to me, put both hands to her mouth and

119

collapsed in a fit of convulsive laughter. It was some minutes before she regained her composure and took solace in a mouthful of *pamplemousse*.

"You have to be joking. There's no way I could..." It was no good, she'd got the giggles again.

I was to see quite a lot of He-she wandering around Brouville with her poodle, not surprisingly she's quite well known locally. A physical education teacher at a Paris school, He-she summers in Brouville and lives in a garage surrounded by gleaming pieces of metal, contraptions that would have not been out of place at the Marquis de Sade's gaff.

I don't want to sound catty, but I've seen some ugly specimens of womanhood in my fifty three years shuffling around this mortal coil and He-she takes first prize, *le medaille d'or*.

When first telling Beth about my plans for the summer she was utterly convinced that copious amounts of scantily clad nubility was going to be falling into Rip-Rap's cockpit and beyond. Far from it, dear reader, far from it. This was Ste Serre not St Tropez you understand, about as far removed from the beautiful ones as it's possible to get, and an 'e' at the end. It was a while before I realised that the 'e' made a difference. It's pronounced 'eh'. So 'Sainte' is 'Santa', just like Christmas. Bloody confusing to a simple Englishman abroad, especially in the middle of the longest and most superb summer I've ever experienced.

Now it's not to say that Brouville doesn't have its moments. Some of the visitors were on the end of a second Marsh glance and one or two of the home-grown variety are worthy of a mention in despatches.

In the main, the Provençal woman would not do too well in a Butlin's beauty contest. True, some have quite passable figures, but I'm quite convinced that the quality control department at the Le Creuset factory has something to do with re-arranging the facial features. They're not so much ugly as interesting faces, like plasticine that's been left out in the sun. I was once told, coincidentally that the original plasticine was re-constituted sewage. I don't know how true that is, but you get my drift.

For my first couple of weeks in Brouville, before the influx of tourists, I was treated to quite a morning eyeful as three of the home-growns arrived at the beach for their daily top-up of UV rays. As is my wont, they were given names for the purposes of personal identification. Fit-Bit, Big Boobs and the Ageing Hippie would put on a display that would've had the talent scout from Raymond's Revue Bar reaching for his cheque book. Father's binocs were pressed into use, as the trio cavorted across the beach, utterly oblivious to the fact that there was somebody watching them, the rod-danglers being far more interested in their floaty things.

I do have to say though that despite my nick-name for her, the Ageing Hippie is in possession of one of the most stupendous rear views it has ever been my privilege to blimp.

There was also a mid-afternoon version of this show, the matinée you might say, when the schoolies arrived back from their studies in Seyne. Although not as spectacular as the morning show, the star of the matinée was indubitably the Bouncing Bombshell. She stopped by at the Café from time to time and despite being not a day over sixteen, is one of the most voluptuous young ladies you can imagine, and when she stops, she's the only thing that does.

I have veered away from the main thrust of this chapter and so, having been reminded of the *Sapeurs Pompiers* by virtue of the fact that not one but two of their helicopters have just glided slowly by, umbilical-like hosepipes dangling expectantly as they scan the woods and forests for illegal Bar-B-Q's to spray, I shall turn my attentions onto these pathetic examples of macho man, and a few macho twats as well. As the latter also double as dogs, they are well within the remit of this episode.

I am a huge admirer of part-time folk who put their own lives at risk for the sake of others, the RNLI being one prime example. To the lifeboatmen of Moelfre I might have owed my life and certainly my pride and joy. They probably knew there was a shit-pipe in the area and I was stuck on it, but that is by-the-by. They did their duty and set sail to rescue a yottie in distress.

However, in their off-duty moments you will not find the brave and fearless of the RNLI strutting their stuff in uniform, sticking their chests out, pushing people out of the way and being generally obnoxious. Far from it — they're more likely to be sitting in the corner of a quiet quayside bar somewhere, imbuing themselves with a feeling of well-being, and of course in mufti. You have little or no chance of knowing that the nice man smiling at you across the bar room has just rescued twenty people from a watery grave and is about to be on the receiving end of the George Medal. No, you'd think, he's just taking the dog for a walk.

The behaviour of the off-duty part-time *Sapeurs Pompiers* however is more attuned to the former description and, as previously mentioned, because the French change things like VAT around I shall change *Sapeurs Pompiers* around, to Pumped-up Soppy Ones.

The gun-loving French macho man has one burning ambition — to be able to strut the streets brandishing a weapon at his hip, legally and legitimately. There is no finer or more superior badge of machoism. The modern day equivalent of the Colt .45 turns heads, demands respect, shows authority and gets women into the sack. Or so they think.

The student riots of 1968 in Paris didn't persuade them otherwise, they still really do believe that wearing a gun turns women on. So they join the Police or *Gendarmes*, after a spell of National Service has given them the taste of gun-toting behaviour and wearing a uniform.

Sadly, some of them are too short, too fat or not quite intelligent enough or have bad eyesight or whatever. So they become part-time Pumped-up Soppy Ones. They get the uniform, the swagger, the respect, the authority, everything but the gun! And that is a big, big problem. The Pumped-up One becomes even more surly, even more brutish, even more obnoxious than his gun-toting counterpart, *le flic*. He has a bigger point to prove and worst of all, he's only part-time. Most of his working life he's a school janitor, a dustbinman, or a road-sweeper, so when evening comes, or the school holidays, whichever is sooner, he can pull on his dark blue sweater with its thin red stripe, his blue serge trousers and heavy rubber-soled calf boots, strap a wide black belt around his usually ample but sometimes inadequate waist and go strut his stuff around the local bars and cafés.

Imagine my delight when One such attired swaggered into a bar in which I was enjoying the odd beer or two and the barman leapt from behind and kissed him. I've never come to terms with men kissing in public. I was a mere youth of 16 when I first saw General de Gaulle do it on telly and, despite having attended public school, I still thought it was a bloody sissy thing to do.

The episode already described of the Pumped-up inflatable moored in my place on the pontoon is a typical example of the kind of arrogance that these despicable pieces of human excrement display. Johnny Foreigner-Bashing is a popular pastime in France, so I take this opportunity to get my own back.

There are other episodes which also serve to illustrate the lack of respect shown to tourists by the part-time Pumped-up Ones. During the course of my first week in Brouville I spent some time familiarising myself with the place and particularly the people. I got to know many by sight and pigeon-holed them, in Sylvan Arnoux's case a whole loft was required.

One such was the village TV man, a spotty, bespectacled youth who bears a remarkable resemblance to the French cartoon character Tin-Tin and whizzes about in a Renault 4 van with huge 'Canal Satellite' stickers on. TV reception is not good in Brouville so most places are hitched up to satellite channels. Tin-Tin was always kept fairly busy but I did notice that, unlike his cartoon counterpart, he didn't have a smile for anyone and despite passing the Café many times he never stopped to shake François' hand, something which nearly everybody who lives in Brouville does.

One evening, turning out of the campsite and heading down to the village for telephone watch, I caught a glimpse of the Renault whizzing through the trees on the road way up behind me. I thought no more about it for the next couple of minutes, but then suddenly there it was filling my rear view mirror, flashing its lights and hooting its horn. I was on a fairly straight bit of road, nothing coming in the opposite direction, so I slowed to let him past, wondering whether some old dear was missing an episode of 'Neighbours' and wanted her aerial straightening. No, the World Cup was on and one of the bars that was showing it had their telly on the blink. He passed me easily enough, there were two of them in the van and a lot of gesticulating and fist shaking went on as if I'd held them up.

I drove into Brouville, pulled up behind the van which was parked outside the only *bar tabac* in the village and went in for some tobacco. I must have been right, the bar's telly had malfunctioned as France were one-all with whoever they were playing. No — two uniformed Pumped-up Soppy Ones were propping up the bar with a couple of beers in front of them. I was on the receiving end of two haughty down-the-nose looks as they lit up and sipped their beers. But not a word was said.

And that brings me neatly to the Macho French driver.

A Frog gets behind a wheel and starts to drive. All goes well until he meets other traffic. It transforms his character. No, sorry, it extends it. I know us Brits are sometimes as bad, and I could tell you some tales about aggressive driving concerning a pal or two having shoved folk beyond their limit and being responsible for 'road rage', as it has become known. Drawing a veil over that, the limp-wristed Macho One becomes even more macho, as he waves his limp wrist, blows his horn, flashes his lights and gesticulates about God knows what. That's when the change takes place, *'rage de la rue'*, 'transfrogrification'. He races along, not just the everyday getting-from-here-to-there, more as if the spirits of Ettore Bugatti and the Marquis de Sade have simultaneously possessed him, racing and raging at the same time.

For the most part that is normal, until a foreign number plate hoves into view. It is simply the fact that to be seen behind Johnny Foreigner is wimpish, pansy, not cool, and if you're seen there, overtake, whatever the circumstances, or pull out the gun and top yourself.

All over France, particularly on the Autoroutes, there are warning signs not to 'tailgate', but they do it anyway, then overtake on either side. We don't have such signs. Maybe it's because it rains a lot in England and the roads are usually slippery and we are used to it. Therefore in France, particularly Provence, the Macho Ones aren't used to it. One thing is for certain, accidents happen. You've just got to look at the plethora of lurid skidmarks and dented barriers on the Autoroutes to confirm that. If I hadn't driven with some circumspection I may have had several bangs, but I didn't.

What I did have was a superb example of Macho banality, when driving into Seyne with the ageing mother, who'd come to visit me for a few days, sitting argumentatively in a dusty passenger seat. She always complains about the state of my car, perhaps because I never clean it. She was having a 'go', as the Volvo slid gracefully into aforementioned town. Behind was a maroon Citroen, no, it was brown, or was it a Peugeot? No matter. The sun, the heat, the mother, or a combination of all these and more things had got to me. That and the car behind.

Three kilometres from town, having seen nothing in my rear-view mirror for ten minutes, there, as I exited a corner, was a maroon or brown bonnet. It inevitably pulled out to overtake. Straight into the path of an oncoming *camion*. Pulling smartly back behind me in what can only be described as a prudent move, he then started flashing his lights. Clearly it was my fault that the smelly truck was coming the other way and had blocked his daring manoeuvre. The Volvo accelerated.

Neither Peugeot or Citroen have yet built a small car that can compete with the ageing Volvo. She can really pick her skirts up when asked nicely and I soon had *le maniac* as a spot in the rear-view mirror. Until I reached the next corner. There, once more, was his bonnet. We were approaching a long series of S-bends so I slowed down to 10mph, just for devilment. Suddenly, I was berated with an endless stream of invective. Macho One was leaning out of the window, waving his limp wrist and shouting at me. We came out of the last bend and the Volvo surged forward once more. This game continued until we reached town where the Volvo once more took its more sedate stance.

Over the sleeping *Gendarme*, across a narrow bridge, around a 90 degree bend and towards a 'Y' junction which isn't really a 'Y', more a left fork and a straight-on bit.

During the months of July and August, Seyne closes its main thoroughfare and pedestrianises the town's main street. The straight-on bit is blocked by galvanised steel barricades and ' No Entry' signs. Imagine my delight as Macho One, his whole upper body now out of the car window, shouting and screaming with both limp wrists waving, went straight on, as the Volvo took the left fork. It was one hell of a clatter, as the rear-view mirror displayed a tangled heap of galvanised steel rods sticking out of the radiator, bonnet and windscreen of a brown or maroon Peugeot or Citroen.

I dropped Mother off at the town square and went to park the Volvo, just as the Pumped-up Soppy One's siren started to wail.

The *Sapeurs Pompiers* carry out all manner of duties in the name of good-deedery.

Apart from putting out fires, they provide the national ambulance service, lifeguards at the lake and other such things. The way in which these duties are carried out, however, is amateurish in the extreme, at least by the part-timers of Brouville, who I'm convinced have had no formal training and simply muddle by using what little common sense they've been blessed with.

I witnessed some shambolic incidents which took place as a result of a siren going off. The wailing sound took its grip as the uniformed Ones rushed about like headless chickens. One particular incident exemplifies a typical call-to-action.

I was just brewing up aboard Rip-Rap one afternoon when the siren sounded, so I popped my head through the hatchway and looked towards the Soppy Ones HQ. Much rushing about was taking place, five or six of them running hither and thither and a lot of shouting was going on. Two of them ran down the pontoon and jumped into the inflatable which had its engine permanently screwed on. The engine was fired up, then the head man shouted to cut it.

Five minutes later a red jeep and trailer with a Dory on arrived at the top of the slipway and reversed into the water. This ensemble is kept handily tucked away in a garage at the back of the village. Thus launched, the Dory came swiftly to the pontoon and was moored up. Ten minutes passed as the boat was loaded with various bits of rescue-type tackle, some of it put in only to be removed as one after another Soppy tried to take charge. The only female Soppy One in the Brouville brigade, a short, dumpy, humourless lump of lard, was shouldered into the water in the confusion and had to be hauled out by three of her colleagues. Eventually, the Dory took to the water, only to return three minutes later because they'd forgotten to take a spare can of petrol.

By this time I'd made my way to the top of the slipway in order to observe the operation and there I met the *Maire*, who explained to me that somebody had fallen off a yacht and sunk without trace. So it didn't really matter that the rescue operation had taken well over twenty minutes to reach this stage. It would've been too late anyway.

I suggested as tactfully as I could to the *Maire* that perhaps it would be a good idea if the Dory was kept permanently rigged and at the ready on the pontoon, because most folk who fall off yachts tend to float for a while. He smiled benignly at me and shrugged, then said it was a good job it hadn't been Rip-Rap that this poor unfortunate had fallen off. His eyebrows were raised and a shudder went up my spine as I headed off to the Café for a beer or two.

Until this summer I had mistakenly thought that the English were tops in the dog-loving world. Believe me, we are Sunday morning pub league compared to the French, who were Premier League and are now World Cup holders.

However, not all the French are macho pansies and most, if not all French families own at least one dog, usually two or more. François' family is one such, just one dog and quite a little tinker is Chaussettes, the French word for 'Socks'.

Of indefinable breed, as most French dogs are, Chaussettes stands a gangly eighteen inches tall, her coat is of longish straggly brown and white hair, she has soulful brown eyes which peer through extraordinary clumps of wispy hair on top of her head and nose and she pants all the time. The pink tongue permanently lollops, and at the other end, the long hairy tail permanently wags. A friendly and loveable creature who wouldn't harm a fly you'd think, but she's a little vixen when other dogs encroach upon her preserve, which is the whole street on which the Café du Soleil sits. Brouville does not boast a pavement anywhere other than the promenade, so François conducts his business on the road, the Café itself being nothing more than a kitchen and bar, a food and drink dispensary.

Oh, and a fly-infested toilet.

I was wandering through the square one evening, shortly before telephone watch, when I espied a magnificent hound outside the Café, a short-haired, jet black Wolfhound, high pointed ears atop a huge squared head with a slavering, droopy jowl. As I walked nearer, the hound became even more awesome. It was the size of a small pony, at least four feet at the haunches with a teat-encrusted underbelly that could have suckled Romulus and Remus well into their late teens. Sir Arthur Conan Doyle must have had this creature's forebears in mind when he penned one of the more famous Holmes adventures.

I sat down at the usual table, Milko brought my *pastis* over and I observed this magnificent creature. It was as docile as a lamb, quietly padding about the road, content to let its owners indulge in jocular banter, which they were doing to some tune. Kids played on the *boules* pitch, shouting, squealing and sliding about on the gravel and the hound cared not a jot. Occasionally the huge mouth would snap at a fly, but that was the most dangerous thing that bothered Baskerville. Until Chaussettes rolled up. Then it was war.

Chaussettes went straight for the hound's throat, having to take a giant leap to get anywhere near. Her teeth sank in as she dangled, front paws a foot or more off the ground, but Baskerville didn't even whimper or flinch, she just stood there and looked at Chaussettes' tail in a bemused way. It was still wagging and that was presumably disconcerting the hound, who obviously couldn't make her mind up whether this was a serious attack or a game. Katrine shot out of the Café and dragged Chaussettes away, bundling the raggedy animal into the back of her car. She returned to apologise to the owners, but so involved were they with jocularity and mirth, nobody had noticed, and the hound didn't say a word. It just carried on padding about and snapping at the odd fly.

Then I suddenly noticed another much, much smaller movement in amongst the kids playing on the *boules* pitch. I'd been so enthralled with the Wolfhound up until then I hadn't noticed the puppy. Neither had the Wolfhound it seemed, for this little creature would have made a tasty mouthful for the mighty beast. Just. It was the size of my hand, a little bundle of black and tan fur and the centre of attraction for the squealing kids, who picked it up, threw it down, tugged it, tweaked it and generally tried to make a mess of the poor mite. It was a resilient little thing, it didn't yap or squeal or snap, but when it was fed up with the attentions of the kids it scuttled under the jocular's table and sniffed the women's feet.

It also sniffed Baskerville's feet and was doing so when the fire engine slewed round the corner and hurtled past the Café, blue light flashing. In a glance, as I dived for the comparative safety of the *boules* pitch, I noticed it was the fat, flabby, female Pumped-up One hunched over the wheel, grinning widely. No sirens, no bells, no horn, no warning. Baskerville leapt for her life as she and the human folk scattered tables and umbrellas and drinks and plates full of food and bottles and ashtrays and chairs, as the speeding Pumped-up Soppy Ones on a variety of transport ranging from trail bikes to the jeep and a Fiat Panda, roared past in pursuit of the fire engine, into the village square and out the other side.

And when all the excitement was dying down and the Café clientele re-arranged themselves and their tables and chairs and drinks and plates and the jocularity started to return, there was a sudden silence as Milko peeled a furry little flat thing off the tarmac and tenderly handed it to the previous owners.

129

Chapter 9

AIX AND PAINS

*In which my bread-loving son Luke pays me a
visit and we meet an Aussie dominatrix and
her son, as well as paying visits to Aix and
other places. Also, more yottin' yarns.*

"Do they still have that scrumptious chocolate bread in France, Dad?"

"Sure do. *Pain au chocolat*, it's called."

"Great! Can I have it every day for breakfast?"

"Yes, of course. You can go to the *boulangerie* and order it yourself. 'Pan chocolar, see voo play' is what you say."

Luke and I were hurtling along the Autoroute la Provençale in the Volvo, on our way from Nice airport to Brouville. He'd come to join me for a week's holiday and I was going to devote myself to his every whim.

"Is there anything special you'd like to do? Anywhere you'd like to see?"

"Nope, not particularly. I'd like to meet your friends at the Café, of course, and do a bit of yottin'. You just do what you usually do. I'm on holiday!"

That morning I'd got up earlier than usual, I think it's fair to say that I was excited by the prospect of having Luke to stay with me. After all it would be the only time I'd see him during my four month sabbatical.

I didn't have to be at the airport until five o'clock and I wondered how I was going to fill the day. Then I remembered that Martine had given me her phone number and said I should go and see her house sometime. She was having a break from the campsite job and would be in most mornings. I telephoned and she said it would be fine, she had an Australian friend and her son staying with her and could I come over for lunch? I groaned inwardly, but said 'yes' anyway.

Martine had told me about her Australian friend, a lady who makes her living by dominating men, 'dominatrix' I believe they're called. Miss Whiplash to you and me. I could think of better companions to share a lunch with, but it might prove interesting.

Martine's house is in a little medieval village called Pont-Eves, opposite the fountain in the village square, and Pont-Eves was on the way to the Autoroute. I got into the Volvo and meandered south. According to my Michelin road map, Pont-Eves is a hill-village, you can tell by all the squiggly lines, so I decided to visit another hill-village on the way, Fox-Amphoux. The name appealed.

It was a delightful little place, everything a hill-village should be, quiet, tiny, picturesque and quaint, with spectacular views, but seriously deficient in one particular aspect. Despite having a hyphen, as all hill-villages should, Fox-Amphoux does not have a bar.

Now if I'm ever going to purchase property in France it is going to have to be within reasonable walking distance of a friendly local. However, in the aspect in which Fox-Amphoux is deficient, Pont-Eves is not.

As I pulled into the village square and spotted the fountain, I saw Martine come out of the *bar tabac* followed by a gangly youth in his early twenties and the most appalling example of middle-aged, menopausal woman it has ever been my misfortune to gaze upon.

Bright red lips and heavily, if somewhat badly applied mascara dominated a face that was full of features, the sort of features you would find on my Michelin road map, somewhere around a hill-village. Unhappily, this face didn't look as if it had any of the features you'd associate with any self respecting hill-village. It didn't look quiet, it certainly wasn't tiny, picturesque never and, as I was about to find out, definitely not quaint. I'll pass over the spectacular views aspect.

"Peetair, you have come."

That was the sort of comment I had hoped to hear uttered from Martine's lips that day, but in her bedroom, the two of us alone,

131

not standing in the village square being gawked at by two Aussie tourists. I bent and kissed her on both cheeks, as is the custom, but all the time my eyes were glued to the apparition behind. I was shortly to be introduced and a few potential names flashed through my mind — Marguerite perhaps, Margaret in reality, but changed to suit the profession. Belinda — Busty Belinda, or Matilda the Waltzing Whiplash. That had potential. I tried to imagine what she'd look like dressed as a French maid, but it was tricky.

My mother once met the real Miss Whiplash, she was after-dinner speaker at a function Mother had attended and after her speak, Mother had introduced herself to Ms Paine and imparted the alarming piece of information that she was in the habit of going to fancy dress parties dressed as a French maid. She does, actually, I've seen the photo, and Ms Paine seemed hugely amused by this fact. She pulled out one of her cards and wrote on the back, 'To Beryl — sorry to have lost one of my best girls. Good luck anyway — Cynthia Paine!' Mother carries it around in her handbag, with the photo of her as a French maid, and pulls them out at all the most inopportune moments.

"Peetair, this is my friend from Australia — Cynthia."

Had to be, didn't it. How stupid can you get, Marsh?

The people of that massive sub-continent have a habit of naming things in a kind of obvious way. Where else but Australia would you find Long White Beach, Great Sandy Desert or Big Snowy Mountains? And even if her real name wasn't Cynthia, it sure as hell was now. The Waltzing Whiplash stepped up and offered me her right hand whilst the left went into her shoulder bag.

"G'day, Pete. Good ter meet yer."

The grip was firm, as you'd expect, but I was nervously watching the left hand and wondering with some trepidation what it was going to re-appear with. It couldn't possibly be a photo of herself dressed as a French maid, now could it? Thankfully it wasn't, it was a handkerchief which was quickly pressed into use in order to remove a huge dew-drop from the end of her hooked beak.

"Sorry 'bout that, Pete. Must be the heat, I guess."

I guessed so too, but before I could say anything the gangly youth stepped up and shook my hand.

"Hi, Pete. I'm Wobblee."

The Australian habit of obviously naming things had struck again, but I did think it was a tad unfair to have christened the poor lad thus.

"Hi, Cynthia. Hi, Wobblee," I said at last.

"Rodney! It's Rodney!" Cynthia was not amused, I could tell by her tone of voice.

"Sorry... Rodney... Right. It must be your accent and you are on my deaf side."

That always turns the tables when I meet someone for the first time. They offer sympathy and start speaking more clearly and deliberately. Cynthia didn't offer any sympathy, but she did speak clearly and deliberately.

"Deaf side, my arse. Don't give me that bullshit, you whingeing Pommie pongo," she screamed.

One or two faces poked out of the *bar tabac* but shot back inside as Cynthia rounded and made off towards Martine's house.

Martine put her arm through mine and said comfortingly, with a smile:

"Come, Peetair, let's have lunch. You like chicken?"

She was spot on. I was.

The house is delightful, exactly as Martine had described it.

Nine rooms on three floors, with solid fuel stoves in all the main rooms and little cubby holes as well. The toilet sits in silent splendour on the first floor landing, no door, no curtain, it just sits there. Fortunately the seat lid was down so I didn't feel too embarrassed as I squeezed past it and followed Martine up to the top floor. There you find the master bedroom and the only piece of decoration in the place. Martine explained that she and her husband had only just finished the restoration of the bedroom when he upped and left and now she was having to sell the house in order to pay him his part of the divorce settlement. She wanted 400,000FF (£40K) for it, she said, but might have to drop. Still, it gave me an idea of what you might get for your money in terms of accommodation. I couldn't work out why the crapper was located on the landing and not in one of the many nooks and crannies though, and I forgot to ask.

We went out into the garden where the Waltzing Whiplash had calmed down and laid out most of the lunch on a modest little wooden table surrounded by four higgledy-piggledy chairs, not one the same. The table is set under a sprawling virgin vine which keeps off the Provence sun and the only other notable growths in the little unruly walled garden are a lychee tree and some bamboo canes. It's a delightful setting for lunch and I set about removing the cork from a bottle of Australian red which Cynthia had brought in the name of getting to know one another.

"Rodney, get a photo of Pete opening the bottle."

I paused in my efforts, in order to give Rodney the chance to do his mother's bidding, and then poured three glasses, the 'sans alcool' Martine was drinking water. She appeared at the garden door with a huge bowl of pasta twirls in tomato sauce, Rodney hacked up the chicken and we feasted the next two hours away in typical Provençal style.

All morning I'd been trying to think of the most tactful way to ask Martine if she would telephone the *Mairie* and find out what had happened to my letter from the *Maire*. It was over a week since my meeting with him and I was concerned that he might have overlooked the urgency of it. We were getting into the tourist season and I was anxious to get going. I needn't have bothered though because during the course of our conversation I was explaining to Cynthia and Rodney about my chartering idea and how useful Martine had been and that all I was waiting for was the letter of authority from the *Maire*.

"What! You have no letter yet? I will ring the *Mairie* now!"

The fiery little thing leapt off her chair, shot through the garden door and into the house. I think it's something to do with the Marseille temperament, or tenacity, or whatever it is.

Whilst she was away I asked Cynthia how she and Martine had got to know each other and she explained that they'd met at Moscow airport four years ago. She had been on her way to Europe from Australia and Martine was going the other way, but they had seven hours of waiting for connecting flights and had got to know each other pretty well. They had kept in touch since by air-mail. I asked if they had by any chance been flying with Aeroflot.

"Jeez, how d'yer guess that, Pete?"

I explained that my daughter had flown to Cuba with Aeroflot and she'd also had a seven hour stop-over in Moscow, in fact come to think about it that was four years ago as well.

"You could've been there at the same time," I finished off by saying.

"So we could. So we bloody well could. Just think of that, Rodney!"

Martine came back with a grin and explained that the *Maire* had been away for a few days but my letter had been typed and the *Maire* would sign it upon his return tomorrow.

"Thanks, Martine. You're a brick," I said, prising the cork out of another bottle.

"What's that funny noise, Dad?" asked Luke as we hurtled along with the sun-roof open.

"*Cicadas.* Noisy little insects, crickets we call them. You've heard them before, surely?"

"Not that I can remember. How big are they?"

"No idea. Never seen one that I know of."

"Have you got them at the campsite?"

"Course. They're everywhere. You just get used to them like the flies and ants."

We were approaching Tourtour and I explained to Luke that this was his Granny's favourite village. She'd been here some years before on a painting holiday. We swung into the village square and pulled up at the red traffic light. The main street of Tourtour is so narrow that traffic has to be controlled by lights, so you sit for three minutes waiting for them to change.

"I've never seen so many tables and chairs," he exclaimed, looking round. "The whole square is just one big pub. Never mind Granny, it'd suit you this place, Dad!"

I smiled. He knows his father.

"Yes, perhaps you're right. We'll come here again, how's that? Take a look round the old village and have a beer, OK?"

"OK."

The next day we went to Aix.

"Did you see that, Dad? She just fell over and nobody took a blind bit of notice".

Alcohol mixed with sun is a dangerous concoction to the young and uninitiated. The pavement had come up to meet this particular young one's head mighty quickly and the passers-by just passed by. Luke was about to go and help her to her feet when the boyfriend hove somewhat unsteadily into view, swigging *vin rosé* from the bottle, pointing at the girl and giggling. She started to giggle too and get to her feet, then she keeled over again and sat in the gutter.

"Come on, Luke. She's only drunk, won't feel a thing — until tomorrow."

We moved on in search of something to amuse the mind of an intelligent seventeen year old, but Aix is sadly lacking in that department. It has a fine market in a broad, tree-shaded street selling all manner of trinkets, paintings and nougat, but we'd done that, listened to a street musician play Luke's party piece on the guitar and had a beer in a gay bar. Now I suggested Les Baux.

"What's that, Dad?"

"A citadel."

"Right. Come on then."

We tanked up the Volvo with 98 octane *Sans Plomb* and left Aix behind us.

"I used to have one of those contraptions," I said, pointing at the huge medieval catapult sitting in splendid isolation on the flat-topped escarpment that is the citadel of Les Baux. "A toy one. It was green and had brown wheels."

"You've still got it, Dad. It's in my toy box with all the jeeps and tanks and tractors. It had an elastic band and you could fire dried peas with it."

I was amazed and suggested we take a photo of Luke standing

by it, but he had other ideas.

"Take one of me sitting where the peas would go. That'd make a better snap."

He climbed up the firing arm and sat in the enormous cup, looking just like a long-haired pea with legs, whilst I clicked away, and then swung down on what would have been the elastic band. There was an enormous twang and clatter as Luke reached the ground faster than he'd intended and the entire contraption collapsed. We tried to put it back together again all to no avail. It would have taken four men to lift one end of the firing arm and fortunately no one else was about. We went for lunch.

I ordered up a beer for me and an Orangina for Luke ('Shake the bottle — wake the taste!') and we gazed at the menu.

"What d'you fancy, Lukey?"

"Sandwich."

French bread in any form, he simply can't get enough of it. I even tried him on a slice or two of the *pain de campagne* and he liked that as well. We ordered two "*sandwichs au jambon*" and sure enough they arrived — two halves of a *baguette* and half a kilo of ham pressed between them, and in long paper bags, so we could munch what we fancied then and take what was left with us. We did, although there wasn't as much left of Luke's as there was of mine, but he finished both of them in the car later.

The main reason for taking Luke to Les Baux was for him to see what's just down the road — Le Cathédrale d'Images. I had visited here on the first day of my four-day tour of Provence in September but had never really explained to Luke what it was all about. It really is something you have to see to experience it and I knew that Luke would enjoy the audio-visual show. Being dyslexic he has erred on the side of graphic images and music, rather than the written word. He'd just finished his first year at Art College and I'd managed to get him three weeks' work experience with my old pal Ben who I'd met at the *Forum Cartoon* and Ben had been very impressed with his natural flair and imagination. So I knew I wasn't going to be disappointed with his reaction to Le Cathédrale.

"It's amazing! Just think, whoever thought this up is a bloody genius. Just imagine, you could do a pop video in here or have your own show. God, that would be amazing..."

He never stopped talking about it all the way back to the campsite and for the rest of the holiday for that matter.

That evening I was sitting outside the caravan sipping wine, smiling about Luke's reaction to the A-V show and mulling over the success of our first day together when Wobblee rodneyed into view on a mountain bike.

"G'day, Pete. How's it goin'?"

"Hi, Rodney. What're you doing here?"

"Oh, Martine suggested we come over here for a couple of days, stay at her place by the campsite reception and perhaps have a sail with you, if that'd be OK."

"Yeah, don't see why not. Luke'll be back soon, he's just gone for a shower, then we're going out for a meal."

Rodney threw down the bike, plonked himself in a chair and lit up. I poured him a glass of wine and we chatted for five minutes until Luke hoved into view and I introduced them. I gave Luke a 50 *franc* note and told him to go to Le Cabanon with Rodney and have a beer or two whilst I freshened up. I'd pick him up later and we'd go into the village.

The boys got on really well together and Luke had met Cynthia, he told me on the way. He really liked Rodney and felt sorry for him having a mother like that. I told him what she did for a living and his eyes shot out of his head.

"Jeez! Now I really feel sorry for him."

We pulled up at the Café and found our way to the usual table, sat down and ordered drink — a *pastis* for me and a beer for Luke. He was very amused at me drinking what he described as 'pansy little cocktails', but he was soon to alter his opinion of the aniseed flavoured rocket fuel. Pappie ambled up to our table.

"*Bonsoir*, Peetair."

We shook hands.

"*Bonsoir*, Pappie. *Il est* Luke."

"*Fils?*"

"*Oui.*"

Pappie shook Luke's hand and I indicated to him that we were about to eat. He wandered off muttering *'Bon appetit'* and Luke asked me who he was. I told him the tale and I shall tell you, dear reader.

I've mentioned before that my French is not up to scratch, far from it. The best I can do is gesticulate, make a few noises and throw in the odd trigger word, but it makes for conversation and general *bonhomie*, whilst I force myself to spend time in bars, and I can order drinks.

Some time before Luke arrived, perhaps a week or so before, I'd been sitting at my Café table and mulling over the day's scribbles when Pappie plonked himself down opposite me and plonked his *boules* pouch on the chair beside him. *'Pastis'*, he'd said, and I nodded thinking that he'd made an observation on the particular beverage I was imbibing at the time. He turned to Milko, made a hand signal and Milko disappeared inside the Café, then reappeared with two glasses of *pastis* and a jug of iced water, one *pastis* for Pappie, one for me. He wordlessly made a slight bow, turned on his heel and returned to his crow's nest outside the Café door. Pappie filled the glasses with water and held his up, saying 'chin-chin'.

Now I had taken drink with François obviously, and the two Brunos from time to time, but generally speaking I kept myself to myself when it came to getting involved with rounds. I had once had the misfortune of joining one of the macho ones, who'd offered me a *pastis* so that he could show me and his mastery of the English language off to his mates. I'd spent half an hour sipping and every five minutes answering the question, 'Peetair, 'ow are yoo?' It was a harmless enough interlude, I suppose, but here I could sense danger.

You can tell simply by looking at Pappie's face that he's not exactly led a monastic life. It's an interesting face, craggy and lined, purple, red and blotchy, and a heavy black moustache flecked with grey. Pappie is a big man, perhaps early to mid-sixties and we'd seen each other around the village, I knew his name, he knew mine and we'd nodded at each other a few times.

Now I was about to find out his life story. It wasn't a conversation as such, more a monologue, but I did interject a few times when I wanted to clarify something he'd said. I was told a couple of days later that Pappie speaks with a thick Provençal accent so that explains why I had some difficulty understanding some of what he said, but I got the drift.

Pappie went to war at an early age, the *Indo-Chine* war, the rehearsal for Vietnam, but he was wounded, quite seriously, and pensioned out of the Army. I'd noticed that Pappie walked with a pronounced limp and when he rolled up his left trouser leg and showed me the damage I quickly realised that it wasn't an affectation; the bullet had smashed his shin bone just below the knee and it had taken the surgeons many months to repair the damage. He was lucky to have kept the leg.

Now it's not a bad life being a *muteille de guerre* in France. You get a medal, a comfortable state pension and folk have to give you their seats on the Paris Metro system, or so it says on the train windows. So when fully recovered from his injury, Pappie set about creating a new lifestyle for himself, drinking, smoking, womanising and playing *boules* being all equal at the top of his agenda of life. At this point in the story I had Pappie down as one of the Macho Ones, maybe a spot of rod-dangling might creep in to the tale, but to my surprise I discovered that he'd never married, never had children that he knew of and therefore had no need for owning a little dog. God alone knows where he got his name from but François thinks it may be a nickname of some kind.

The years crept by and the life-style eventually took its revenge. Seven-day-a-week drinking, smoking, womanising and *bouling* came to an end when six years ago Pappie had a heart-attack and a by-pass operation. It was not difficult for me to misunderstand this part of the tale — he unbuttoned his shirt and showed me this scar as well.

So, a new life-style had to be devised. It would not include smoking and women, the *boules* cut to twice a week on doctor's orders, but the drinking was to continue. *Pastis* kept the blood

140

circulating, Pappie informed me as he ordered our fourth one. By now I'd lost track of who was paying for all this, but I cared little, I'd warmed to the company of this gentle giant and figured that it'd all be alright in the end. But why had he picked on me that evening? Maybe he'd bored everybody else in the village with his life story and was casting his net wider, who knows?

Then came the revelation. (In France, they usually have revolutions. Apparently the World Cup had cost the taxpayers so much that had France not won there would have been a revolution).

Pappie tapped the side of his nose conspiratorially and leaned across the table. He is a *boules* hustler. During the summer season he tours around the region taking part in the many *boules* tournaments which are staged in the bigger towns, some of them for quite big money. Pappie wins the money, or large slices of it, then returns to Brouville to rest up and spend his winnings on *pastis,* in order to keep the blood pumping, you understand.

There was some blood pumping done that night, I can tell you, judging by the next day's headache, and it had cost me not a *franc.* That day Pappie had won.

"Well, Dad," said Luke, as I finished the tale and he glanced over at the huge head and shoulders sitting a few tables away. "Your kind of dude. Mine too."

The next day dawned boringly bright, so bright in fact that I was forced to pull out my Liam Gallagher sunglasses. I attached them to the dayglo yellow elastic thingy that holds them to my head whilst yottin' and Luke and I set off for the pontoon to prepare Rip-Rap for an afternoon's sail. Not before Luke had had his daily belt of *pain au chocolat* though, washed down with a mug-full of Choky chocolate. He really does love the things.

I prefer the standard *croissant* with Robertson's Golden Shred marmalade which I love, so much so I'd taken three jars of the stuff to France with me just in case I couldn't buy it locally. Good job, all I could find on the shop shelves was jam, jam, and more jam. All flavours except orange.

*

"OK, Luke. Pull her up, fast as you can," I shouted towards the bows, yanking hard on the jib-sheet and pulling the headsail out on the roller-reefing.

Luke got the anchor onto the deck, the wind caught the sail and we were off, sailing close and parallel to the rocky shore. Luke came back to the cockpit after stowing the anchor and we threw in an immediate tack. Rip-Rap powered away from the shore and we headed out of the lagoon, past the village and towards the main part of the lake.

"OK girls, you can come up now."

Luke and I had motored over to the campsite beach, picked up Martine, Cynthia and Rodney, and I'd sent Martine and Cynthia down to the cabin just to get them out of the cockpit and give myself more room to manoeuvre. Rodney had stayed topsides just in case I needed somebody to pull something, but it all went smoothly enough.

"You looked worried, Peetair, I could tell with your face. Why?" Martine asked, as she came up the companionway and sat down in the cockpit.

"Simple, old girl. Wind against the shore. Always tricky in a sailboat and I don't like scratching my pride and joy. Not in public anyway."

Martine was taking a real interest in yottin' and I was pleased. This would be her fourth trip with me and its good to share something you love so much with an enthusiastic learner. A bit like sex, I suppose. I smiled into her deep brown eyes and she smiled back, a wide smile that showed off her whiter than white teeth. She was also getting used to my humour.

"Hey, this is great! Rodney, get a photo of me with Pete."

The moment was shattered as the Antipodean lump of lard oozed up the companionway into the cockpit and gave her first order of the day. I quickly realised that I was in danger of loosening my grip on just who was in charge here.

"OK, Luke. Ready about. Sit over there, Cynthia."

We tacked and Luke looked quizzically at me. He knew it was a completely unnecessary manoeuvre, but I just smiled back at him and glanced down at Cynthia, then back at his face. He grinned and nodded in an understanding way. We tacked again. And again, and again, and again until finally we were out of the lagoon and onto the lake. It's a while since Luke and I had sailed properly together, but it all came back to him fairly quickly and he was soon in the rhythm of things.

"Hey, there's more to this sailing business than you think," said the Waltzing Whiplash. "You guys are pretty good. You work well together."

'So we bloody well should,' I thought, but just smiled.

"So you are happy man now, Peetair. You have your letter from the *Maire*," Martine said.

I had. Rodney had brought it round to the caravan that morning and I'd read and understood most of it, but there was something about taxes that I was unsure of.

"Would you read it for me, Martine? I need to understand it all."

She did, and as she did my heart sank once again.

It wasn't permission to charter, he wanted to see something in writing from the *Affaires Maritime* people in Paris that said I could charter with his permission and he also said I had to pay a large proportion of my earnings in local taxes.

"So I still can't charter! What's with you French, Martine?"

"It is simple. Nobody wants to take the responsibility. If you have an accident, somebody drowns, then the finger will point at the *Maire*. He is the one who gave you the permission so it will be his responsibility. Also it is his job to make sure everybody earning money in his *Commune* pays tax. We are socialist country, and besides, there is much jealousy of you in Brouville."

I looked at her incredulously.

"Jealousy? Jealous of what, for Christ's sake? I'm just a guy trying to make a crust out of the tourists, like everybody else in Brouville. Why won't they let me?"

"It is not that. They don't understand. They think you are some rich Englishman come here with your lovely yacht to take business away from them. I know it's not true, but that's what they think."

I was dumbstruck. And very down again, but I wasn't going to let it spoil the day.

"Come on Luke. Use the swimming ladder."

Luke's pink face huffed and puffed as he tried to pull himself out of the water and up the side of the boat.

"I would, but there's a bloody Frog in the way!"

Martine was standing on the transom at the top of the ladder preparing herself for a dive. She turned to me with a smile and said:

"He's a cheeky one, your son."

Then she launched herself into the greeny-blue water and surfaced about 20 yards away.

"There, Luke. There's no bloody Frog in the way now," she shouted and swam away.

We'd thrown the hook down close to a lee shore as the wind was getting up from the south and everybody wanted a swim. Martine had already had one, right in the middle of the lake. She just peeled off her T-shirt and dived in. It was a mite alarming for the Skipper, but good Man Over Board drill.

My mind went back to Plas Menai as I pushed the tiller over, ordered a tack and turned Rip-Rap onto a broad reach towards the little face in the water. The little face loomed larger and the little mouth opened and let out a scream.

"Hey! You going to run over me!"

I remembered what Skipper John had said. 'Don't approach the M.O.B. too fast — it frightens them seeing what appears to be a huge boat coming straight at them'. I freed off the jib-sheet, de-powering the headsail and Rip-Rap slowed instantly. We drifted up to the little head and came up alongside. Martine made it up the ladder and off we went again.

I thought once more about what a valuable weekend that was and silently thanked young Paul for suggesting that I do the ICC course.

"What do you think of greeny-blue water sailing, Luke?" I asked, as we sailed back towards Brouville.

The others had all had a swim, we'd had a picnic of ham and

cheese sandwiches and a few beers. It had been a really pleasant afternoon in the warm sunshine with a cooling breeze. Even the *Gendarmes'* boat had paid us a visit. They'd motored slowly around Rip-Rap as she lay at anchor and once around the stern they waved and made off. Martine said they had been checking that I had an electric motor and once they'd confirmed that I had, they left. I was to curse that electric motor later.

"Its great, Dad. Real yottin', not like getting piss wet through motoring up and down that grey river!"

I roared with laughter and remembered last year when every time Luke and his pal Joe came yottin' with me we just seemed to motor up and down the Straits from Menai Bridge to Caernarfon and back. And it had always rained. Occasionally we'd had a sail or two out, like the memorable and only time I beat Duncan and Rufus. We'd come through the Swellies from Port Dinorwic to Menai Bridge and Dunc shouted over,

"Last one in The Gazelle buys!"

He won that time, but as we dropped the moorings to head back I shouted,

"Last one in The Mostyn buys!"

It was easy. My mooring, despite being the other side of the tidal stream is considerably nearer to the pub than Duncan's and Rip-Rap has a fin keel whereas Rufus is a bilge-keeler, the fin being faster up-wind. We were on our second pints when he arrived.

The memory of that day, probably the only time it didn't rain when Luke and Joe were with me, only served to remind me that on the Straits and around Anglesey and the North Wales coast, at least you have somewhere to aim for, somewhere to sail to and do something. On the Lac de Ste Serre there isn't really anywhere except Brouville. Sainte Serre and Les Gaps are just tourist beaches and you daren't leave a boat at anchor for fear of returning to find it swamped with dripping wet kids using it as a diving platform. So you go round the lake and back to where you started.

It's pleasant enough though.

The wind was still up as we tacked off Sainte Serre beach and turned towards Brouville on the other side of the lake. It was a shy reach with about 20-25 knots of wind and Rip-Rap relished it. With having five people on board I was able to sheet in the full rig, without reefing, and get her tramping along, whilst staying fairly flat in the water. Six knots came up on the log, then seven and seven point five. It was the best yott I'd had to date and the wind kept up as we creamed into the lagoon and whizzed past the Café. Then I turned in towards the pontoon and went around to the far side and my mooring. I dropped the sails and turned the motor on, but the wind was still too strong and dead on the nose. We couldn't stem it.

I was bloody furious, cursing the pansy little electric motor, the Effin EDicts, the *Gendarmes*, the Pumped-up Ones and, for good measure, the rod-danglers.

I had to let Rip-Rap drift back with the motor switched off, pull out the headsail and make a valiant attempt at getting somewhere near the pontoon under sail. Luke went up to the pulpit as I slotted her neatly into someone else's mooring. Sod it, I thought. I'm buggered if I'm going to mess about any more. We severely upset a rod-dangler, who'd staked his claim on the vacant patch of water, tied up and the others headed for the nearest bar, as Luke and I tidied and locked up.

I watched in horror as another yacht made towards the pontoon and realised that Rip-Rap was in his spot. As he approached I recognised that it was the *Club Nautique* boat with one of the young instructors at the helm. I breathed a sigh of relief as he almost casually sailed straight into my spot as if he was on a Laser. They're bloody good, these youngsters.

"D'yer like steak, Pete? Rump steak?"

"Certainly do, Cynthia."

"How about you, Luke, you like rump steak?"

"Do I!"

We were sitting on Le Bouchon terrace, the nearest bar to the pontoon where the others had found a table and ordered ale. Everybody was thirsty, so the tramp up the village to the Café had been abandoned in favour of this watering hole. The Skipper and

First Mate had joined the rest of the crew and Luke idly looked at the menu whilst sipping his ice cold beer and noticed with glee that they did pizzas. He loves pizzas, it's just another form of bread, so I promised him we would come here one evening. Then he went to the toilet.

It was five o'clock and Luke goes to the toilet at five o'clock, always has, as long as I can remember. Like Mr Goodbody's wall turning pink, you can set your watch by it, but he was having difficulty with the French toilets. He'd already inspected a few and dismissed them as being 'growlers' (the typical French holes-in-the-ground) or having too many flies (the Café du Soleil), no seats (Le Camping), no toilet paper or whatever. He returned triumphantly from Le Bouchon toilet and, with a broad grin, announced that this was by far the best toilet in Brouville, possibly all of France. We would definitely be coming back.

"Good. Then that's settled," announced Cynthia, once again on dry land and therefore in charge. "You'll come round to Martine's place and eat with us tonight."

It was a command, there was no doubt about it.

"But I only have three chairs!" wailed Martine, pitifully.

"So have I," I said.

"You have got these from Stefan?"

My first day at the campsite I had complained that I had nothing to sit on outside the caravan, just to add to my whinges about no gas, no electricity, no water and everything else. Martine had suggested I ask Stefan who runs Le Cabanon. I did, and he'd let me have one of his plastic patio chairs on permanent loan.

"One from Stefan, and two I found in a *poubelle*," I announced proudly.

Martine collapsed with laughter and was speechless.

"What in God's name is a bloody *poubelle* when it's at home?" screeched the Waltzing Whiplash.

"You going to tell her, Martine? Or shall I?"

It was going to have to be me, Martine was helpless. I suppose it was the thought of the rich Englishman with his beautiful yacht lifting discarded camping chairs from *poubelles* that had got her going.

"Dustbins, dearie. Those bloody great green plastic wheelie bins that are sprinkled liberally around the *Commune de Brouville*. Its amazing what you find in them."

Cynthia joined Martine in helpless mirth, even Luke and Rodney appreciated the funny side.

We took the two folding camp chairs, refugees from the *poubelle*, to Martine's that evening and a good time was had. I also took wine, a three litre flagon of the up-market local *Vin de Table Rouge* purchased for 60FF (I was on the good stuff now), Cynthia provided the steaks, Rodney and Luke did their hunkers on the communal Bar-B-Q whilst being very amused by the karaoke which was going on at Le Cab, Martine got seriously chatted up by Frans, a Dutch cyclist who was staying on the site and came over to join us, and the next day was arranged. I was to regret it.

"It's just like Five Mile Road, isn't it, Rodney. You know Five Mile Road, Pete?"

"I've told you Cynthia, I've never been to Australia."

"Right. Well this is just like Five Mile Road. It's a road that winds its way up to an old mining village in Queensland, very quaint."

"And five miles long, I'll bet."

"Yeah, that's right! How'd'yer guess?"

We were driving up the Gorges du Durance towards Guillestre, a must for any sightseer who visits the region, and I suppose you could classify Cynthia, Rodney and Luke as sightseers. Me, I was a local by now, the tour guide, hoodwinked by my dear little female French friend the night before.

I now realised that Martine had tired of the friendship that had been cemented in Moscow airport and had decided to cleverly off-load her Antipodean charges onto the male half of the now dissected Marsh family. Had I offered to take Cynthia and Rodney with us? I know not. The local *Vin de Table* had worked its magic and seen me metaphorically under the local table.

So here we were and I was cursing Martine up one side of the Gorge and down the other. We wandered around Brigance until we found a bar and did the same thing in Guillestre. Luke found me a *Cave* where the sadly depleted stock of *Vin de Table* was replenished, another three litre flagon, this time for 49.50FF, and we headed back down the Gorge towards Pruniers.

"Ooooh, could we swim down there, Pete? It looks lurverley."

Wordlessly, I pointed the Volvo at a convenient parking spot and pulled up.

"Rodney, get the camera. You coming Pete?"

I replied that I would not be taking a swim, thank you very much for asking Cynthia, I needed to take a pee and I'd see them all in fifteen minutes. I was mightily angry with the Antipodean lump of lard and needed time to cool down. It was an hour later, as Luke and I had managed to give them the slip and were sitting alone in a bar over-looking the picturesque village square of Pruniers when I finally gave verbal vent to my anger.

"What, for Christ's sake, is going on, Luke? What's it all about?"

"No idea, Dad. I thought maybe it was something you'd arranged with Martine."

"Me? No bloody chance! I've got you for three more days and that's that. I'm not having our time together fucked up by that fat, ugly example of Antipodean debauchery. Today's been bad enough for God's sake. You wait till I see Martine. Just bloody wait..."

"OK, Dad. OK! It wasn't Martine's idea, OK? It's obvious now, Cynthia wants me to go with them as company for Rodney, right?"

It was somewhere between Guillestre and the swim that I overheard Cynthia, sitting in the back with Luke, say to him that she'd persuaded Martine to take him with them to her house the following day and then to visit Marseille. 'You ever been to Marseille, Luke?' I couldn't believe what I was hearing and the road at that point needed some serious concentration if I didn't want to end up doing a repeat of the end sequence of 'The Italian Job', so I kept schtum and decided to go into this thing later.

The later was now, and my blood was still boiling, but rapidly simmering down as I gulped at a half litre of ice cold *panaché*.

"Yeah, guess you're right. So she persuaded Martine and Martine said 'yes'?"

"Reckon."

"OK, let's forget it. Unless you want to go with them, of course. Do you?" I was smiling when I said it. Luke just smiled back and sipped his beer.

Cynthia and Rodney finally located us and we headed back to the car park. I was suddenly seized with the notion that folk may think that we were an item, a family unit; husband, second wife, son and stepson, so I put a spurt on and was sitting in the car rolling a fag when they arrived. I'd also made the decision that, whatever happened or was suggested, Luke and I would spend the day on Rip-Rap tomorrow, alone.

At last, I thought, the Waltzing Whiplash had come up against one man she couldn't dominate. Pommie pongo, indeed!

"For Christ's sake, Luke, get the boat-hook and fend us off."

I'd decided to try and leave the pontoon under sail, practice was required for this manoeuvre and it was better to practice with someone else I could trust on board. Also someone who wouldn't laugh too much if I got it wrong and wrong I had got it.

Rip-Rap had turned arse about face and was inexplicably heading straight for a reef some 30 yards from the pontoon. I looked up at the sails and beyond to the wind indicator at the top of the mast. It was pointing one way, the sails had other plans. Sailing on Le Lac can be like that, sometimes the wind swirls. We were about five yards from the rocks doing a steady three knots when suddenly Rip-Rap answered to the helm and switched direction. Two huge sighs of relief issued forth and Luke returned to the cockpit, stowed the boat-hook and sat down.

We were heading past the pontoon and out towards the lake when he said:

"A bit 'Gazzish' that was, Dad."

"You're not kidding!"

Luke has been with Gary and me many times when the Big Knob takes short cuts around the numerous headlands which Anglesey has to offer. This involves many tacks, half of which are taken within touching distance of a rock-face. We've never hit one to date, but that had been the closest call yet.

We tried to get into my favourite little lagoon which I'd pointed out to Luke from the road and was eager to show him, but the wind was once again not in our favour. We were a hundred yards away on an awkward twisty beat when I glanced over towards the lagoon and saw that the water even in that sheltered spot was quite disturbed, indicating wind. It would have been foolish to even try. I'd had my fill of Big Knob-like manoeuvres for one day, so I turned and we headed for another, bigger lagoon which, if I guessed correctly, would have a lee shore off which to anchor. I was right, down went the hook, up went the boom tent and we cracked open a couple of bottles.

A huge gulp later, I grimaced and looked at the label: 'Sans alcool'. I looked at Luke, he just grinned back, his eyes squinting against the bright sunlight.

"It's not even LA — it's NO bloody A!"

"I know, Dad, I thought you did too. You picked them up in the shop."

His French was obviously improving.

"And you didn't say anything?"

"Nope. I never know what you're going to drink next with all those shandies and pansy little cocktails."

I'd had a feeling it was going to be one of those days as we'd headed for the rocky outcrop at the start, and it wasn't over yet.

Luke went out in the dinghy tethered to a long mooring line and took some photos of Rip-Rap lying at anchor. I left him there for a while, to stew, whilst I searched every locker on the boat for something with alcohol in it, all to no avail, apart from half a bottle of White Spirit and I haven't stooped that low yet. It was a good job, as it happens. The wind got up and the anchor started dragging, so I pulled Luke and the dinghy in, de-rigged the boom tent, hoisted the main and we hauled up the now fast dragging anchor. I yanked out the headsail and pointed as close to the wind as I could get her, out of the lagoon.

Out in the middle of the lake the wind was reminiscent of two days ago, but there had been five of us then, only two today. Luke sat out on the rail and I sat up as far as I could whilst still being able to reach the tiller and the main-sheet jammer, the sheet I held constantly in my hand.

The wind moderated for a while and Luke came down to the cockpit to put a T-shirt on. Then it hit us. The most God Almighty gust I'd experienced thus far, it must have been 40 knots or more. I was standing on the side of the leeward cockpit locker, no chance of uncleating the main-sheet, which I'd dropped along with the tiller in order to hold onto something more substantial. Luke was pinned by his own body-weight against the leeward guardrail, half in and half out of his T-shirt and the water. The cross-trees, however, were completely in the water. Then the gust eased and Rip-Rap came shuddering up again. The dripping sails powered up and we were off. Luke straightened himself out, pulled the other half of his wet T-shirt on and said,

"Think I'd better stay up on the rail, Dad."

"Not a bad idea, son, not a bad idea."

I was reminded of a comment made by Chrissie's father, the chap who'd won the Fastnet all those years ago when I announced to him that I was taking Rip-Rap to Le Lac. 'Very beautiful, but very boring, I've been told'. His informant is correct on one count.

The landing under sail was good though, I'd been rehearsing it in my mind ever since watching the *Club Nautique* instructor the other evening. Even Luke congratulated me.

That night we went to the Café for a celebratory steak and then back to the campsite to say G'bye to the Antipodeans. It was good to be alive, and on our own again!

"I like your idea of sightseeing, Dad. Drive around for a bit, park up, find a bar and watch the world go by."

It was our last day together, the last hour of the last day, and we were sitting at a bar table on the harbour chicane of the Monaco Grand Prix circuit. Luke had encapsulated, in those few words, just what had been done.

We had left Brouville early, Luke having said his goodbyes at the Café the night before, driven to Nice and along the promenade, then made our way along the coast road to Eze, where Lara and Cris had been a couple of months before. They had both been mightily impressed with the quaint little village, so I'd decided it must be worth a visit. It was. We'd sat on the terrace of the Chateau d'Eze restaurant, perched on top of a sheer cliff with its spectacular view of St Jean Cap Ferrat, 1300 feet below and across the bay, and enjoyed a lunch of *Croque Monsieur* for Luke ('the poshest ham and cheese toastie I've ever had!') and *Salad Nicoise* for me. We had at least a couple of hours or more before Luke had to be at Nice airport, so I asked him if he'd like to see Monte Carlo.

"Would I! How far is it?"

"About three miles," I replied, so we returned to the car and set off.

A quick lap of the circuit, well I say quick, it took perhaps ten or so minutes longer than the likes of Damon Hill (we got stuck behind a bus), then we parked up on the Harbour front, just by the swimming pool.

The sheer opulence of it all, as we wandered slowly around the Harbour yott-spotting, got to Luke and he said he felt very uncomfortable. It is a far cry from Macclesfield and I suggested that a beer might make him feel a bit easier, so we parked our bums at the aforementioned bar table.

I ordered and as we awaited ale, I regaled Luke with stories of old about famous racing incidents that had taken place at this very spot, starting with Alberto Ascari's dive into the harbour somewhere in the mid-fifties and culminating in a spectacular crash during this year's race. Luke sadly does not share my love of the sport and was mighty thankful when the ale arrived. Mighty impressed with the measures too.

"Proper pints!" he exclaimed.

As mentioned before, I know how to order drinks, and there wasn't too much froth on top of these pints.

"Bet they cost a fortune," he added.

I showed him the bill. £2.50 a pint. He kept it as a souvenir, to show his mates.

The time passed quickly, too quickly and we left for Nice airport which I knew from the January trip takes about half an hour.

Beth, Gaz and I had partaken of Sunday lunch in Monte Carlo, I'd had roast beef and two veg, the others stuffed themselves full of tarts and we'd only just made the plane in time.

Luke loved the drive through the catacomb of old tunnels which takes you out of the *Principauté* and towards the Autoroute ('Just like a James Bond movie') and we headed for the airport. We checked him in and hugged goodbye. I hate prolonged partings, so I left him at Passport Control and headed back to the Volvo.

The journey back to Brouville along the Autoroute passed in a blur. I'm not ashamed to say I was crying. It had been a memorable week which had passed all too quickly and the pain of parting, as well as the heart-ache of knowing that I wouldn't see him for more than two months, just got to me.

I resolved to have *pain au chocolat* for my breakfast each day from then on. With Golden Shred, of course.

Chapter 10

HOLIDAY CAMP FEVER

In which I tell of the high season invasion
of Brouville by thousands of the world's
great unwashed.

"All human life is there," my mother had once said, in one of her more philosophical moments, but I don't think she was referring to Brouville at the time. It may have been Butlin's Pwllheli — we used to pass it a lot when I was a kid, on our way to and from the family holidays. In fact all my life I've passed Butlin's Pwllheli, on the landside and the seaside, but I've never been inside. It's always been hard for me to imagine just what it's like inside. I think maybe now I've got a pretty good idea.

I'd seen Brouville in September, January, March and June. Now I was about to see it in July and August.

When I'd first arrived, all my new friends had time for a drink and a chat, it was idyllic, the life-style I'd craved for and thought about as England dripped its chilly way through winter and dripped on into spring. Happy hours spent in warm sun, cold ale and merry banter.

As July wore on all that changed. It didn't happen suddenly, nothing in Brouville, or the rest of France for that matter, ever does. It just kind of crept up on me, a slow dawning that this was what I'd come to the place for and this was reality.

Subtly the village changed, shops opened where I hadn't realised there were any, I'd just thought they were lock-up garages. A covered stage was erected on the municipal car-park at the top of the slipway, in order to accommodate the various entertainments which were to be on offer. The Tourism office, until now firmly closed, started to open its doors of a morning and the *boulangerie* stayed open all day. Worst of all, I had to book a table if I wanted to have a meal at any of the half dozen restaurants and cafés. This was a serious blow in the life of spontaneity to which I had accustomed myself. It was a large part of everyday life to be able to drop everything and go some place and eat, any time of the day or night. Now I was having to plan each meal hours if not days in advance, which took a lot of the fun out of life.

And there wasn't a bar as such, not one you could lean against and natter with your pals. For a start, your pals were too busy extracting *francs* from folk and all the bars had been converted to food and drink dispensaries. If you attempted to lean against one you very quickly got shoved out of the way by histrionic waiters and waitresses. It was not conducive to relaxation. So the agenda for life had to be fine-tuned once again.

Perhaps the largest crowd of the great unwashed it has been my privilege to be part of was at the Reading Festival two years previously, an estimated quarter of a million of them. Luke, then only fifteen, had pleaded with me and I'd taken him.

So there I was, probably the oldest by a good 20 years, enjoying the atmosphere, some of the music and the shouts of 'Bollocks!' every time it started to rain. I heard a lot more 'Bollocks!' than music during the four days of Festival fun, but my bald head and white beard made for quick service at the bar.

"For God's sake get that old geyser at the back a drink before it's too late!" would come the shout.

Luke did the Festival with some pals last year and this year they went to roll about in the Glastonbury mud for four days, so when he saw Le Camping Municipal and the caravan, which I'd run down as much as possible during telephone chats before his visit, he thought it was Center Parcs. Then again, he was in Brouville during the tourist season build-up and it was only after he'd left that I began to observe the changes that were taking place.

The water level in the lake started to drop, at least six feet in a week. Was it because the folk in Marseille were suddenly drinking more? No, it was in order to make the beaches wider to accommodate the influx of grockles, many of whom would have suffocated had the EDF not lowered the water, the surface of which was taking on the look of an orange and white plastic logjam, as the hitherto idle pedaloes got rented out. The rod-danglers on the pontoon grew in number, doubling, trebling and then quadrupling, and what little space there was left provided stepping stones for the hordes of screaming bathers who charged up and down dripping wet through before hurtling themselves at the water once more.

Working aboard Rip-Rap became unbearable, despite the occasional appearance of bikini-clad nubility, so I stayed in the haven which was Le Camping Municipal and only ventured onto the pontoon if I was going out for a sail. In fact, I was spending much less time in Brouville village altogether, only visiting the shops for my daily supply of sustenance, which had replaced eating out and was taken at Le Camping. I had become a virtual hermit with nobody to talk to and take ale with, but most importantly, nobody planning to visit. I'd openly discouraged any of the people who'd said they might come to see me from doing so during July and August because I would be too busy chartering to give them much time.

The complex legalities I was faced with as well as the disproportionate cost of doing what I wanted to do made me decide to drop the idea altogether and to see the summer season through by burying myself in work. That's not to say that I didn't take folk out for a sail, I did, but they were all English or English-speaking, and I read the riot act to them before they came anywhere near the pontoon and Sylvan Arnoux, who had his beady eye on me, without a doubt.

"Friends!" I'd say to him. "*Mes amis*," and he'd nod a trifle suspiciously.

Could one Englishman abroad have that many friends?

I suppose by doing my chartering in this way I had at least some control over who did and didn't come yottin'. My greatest fear of the whole project, apart from the wrath of the French authorities, was the type of person I might have aboard Rip-Rap. The Waltzing Whiplash had been bad enough but I'd managed to keep her under some sort of control, because she was on board by invitation and thick as two short goannas. Fare-paying folk would be different. There's no telling what examples of the unwashed I'd have to put up with, ordering me about and making a general nuisance of themselves.

So my time spent at Le Camping was partly taken up with observing each new influx and weighing up whether they were worth approaching or not.

To this end, I spent some time each afternoon at Le Cabanon, positioned right next to the campsite reception, where I could take ale with Stefan and/or Stephanie, his wife, and idly check out the newcomers as they checked in.

This was pleasant enough, it was quiet during the day with all the grockles baking on the beach and conversation was what I was lacking, although talking with the male Stef was not easy. He spoke no English and only wanted to talk football. The female Steph, however, was a completely different saucepan full of *suppions*. An attractive yet fearfully thin redhead, her English is broken but largely understandable, and she showed an interest in yottin', enough for me to rashly invite her out for a sail one day.

That's another story, and I'll have to wait and see whether I'm bold enough to tell it.

You see huge slices of other people's lives on a campsite, nothing much is secret.

Every family row, the eating and drinking habits, personal hygiene fetishes and foibles, it's all there to see and hear.

I've spent much time on European campsites, mostly in the course of my work. For some years I'd had one of the larger camping holiday companies as a client, so a great deal of product familiarisation took place. That and the occasional holiday which was taken with said company at reduced rates. As a sort of employee I was allowed to take advantage of the company cancellation scheme, whereby you took somebody's cancelled booking at a hugely discounted rate.

But the best perk by far was when I remade the company's promotional video. This involved visiting and filming seventeen different sites all across Europe and I had been allowed to take the then Mrs Marsh and Luke with me. It was a superb three weeks which Luke still talks about and calls the 'European Tour'.

So, Le Camping Municipal, Brouville held no particular fears for me in terms of the sort of people I would encounter, or so I thought. The difference between the sites I'd previously visited and Brouville was dramatic. Instead of late registered Volvos, BMWs, Rovers, Jaguars and the like, I was now surrounded by clapped-out old bangers and an assortment of Rent-a-Vans, and that perhaps defines for you the social strata I'd now entered. A couple of stars missing off the sign at the entrance and the tattooist's art being much in evidence.

At least my caravan was positioned right at the far end of the site, which is situated on a wooded headland jutting into the lake. Apart from six permanent caravans, mine being one, there were six small emplacements for transient travellers who stayed for one or two nights mostly. It was fairly peaceful most of the day, with the main pathway to the beach in a valley running parallel to our service road, which was effectively a cul-de-sac. Behind the row of caravans was a steep, rocky, tree-covered slope which led down to a high chain-link fence and the Riding School beyond.

For the month of August therefore it became my haven, the hermit's retreat, and provided me with a crow's-nest from which to observe the ways of the unwashed *'en vacances'*.

One lady who stayed with her husband at the next door caravan for a few days just had to go to the toilet block at four every morning. I was woken by the sound of the awning zip, four feet from my slumbering head, which she not only undid, but did up again upon leaving and returning. It's a fearsomely loud noise at that, the stillest time of the day when even the *cicadas* have a nap, and once awake I found it difficult to get off again. Perhaps she was getting her own back for my snoring.

This same lady had a high-pitched, piercing voice which disturbed thought patterns during the day and her husband talked like a barking Alsatian. Fortunately neither she nor her husband ever laughed — they were Belgian — and all-in-all I was glad to see the back of them.

Then there was the Dutch couple who camped opposite. I not

only saw the back of them, I saw every other little bit, of her particularly. I've rarely seen such blatant exhibitionism. Milko's winter waiting job is in the Alpine ski resorts and he assures me that it is the Dutch who lead the way in the European Sexual Depravity Stakes.

I have absolutely no reason whatsoever to doubt him.

The German couple next door to the Dutch however were the complete opposite.

They arrived a couple of days after the Dutch and spent a large part of their first afternoon pitching camp and what a camp. It took up two emplacements.

Around the front of the huge frame tent, commodious enough to accommodate a family of eight, Adolf (yes, he had a Hitler moustache!) and Eva erected an enormous windbreak which I nick-named the Berlin Wall. It was not to provide shelter from the prevailing wind, that came from the other direction, it was to keep the prying eyes of us other campers away from whatever it was they got up to in the Chancellory. I doubt it was much, they seemed an extremely prudish couple and the most daring garment worn by either was Adolf's pair of navy blue knee-length shorts, with creases and turn-ups.

He was wearing these when the Mistral blew up late one afternoon, sitting in secluded isolation in his camp chair, legs crossed, eyes closed, as his head nodded, in time no doubt to some Wagnerian dirge emanating from the headphones of his personal CD player. Eva was in the tent, ironing his shirts with her back to the entrance.

How do I know all this? How am I able to paint for you such a precise picture of what was going on in East Berlin? The wind gusted and Adolf nodded on, completely unaware that the Berlin Wall had collapsed.

When Wagner's finest piece had climaxed and Adolf's eyes finally opened, he quickly realised that his private *reverie* had gone public, shot out of his chair and, with Eva's help, hastily re-erected the thing. But it happened again, and again, and again. That's the Mistral for you.

The whole of the next morning was spent dismantling the major part of Berlin and they left for more sheltered climes.

In their place that evening, and by way of another complete contrast, we had a Franco-Chinese family, mother, father and two teenage children, one of each. Their ageing Citroen BX19 pulled to a halt as I went into the caravan and poured myself a *pastis*, with a liberal dollop of well water. I'd taken to filling my plastic bottles daily at the well in Brouville village, the water was pure and sweet-tasting, and free.

Upon exiting the luxury bungalow and strolling around the terrace, glass in one hand, tailor-made cigarette in the other, I observed a two-man Eskimo sort of tent, the type much favoured by back-packers, which had been erected next to the Citroen opposite and the Chinese had disappeared, presumably to the toilet and wash block. I marvelled at the speed with which this feat had been accomplished and was just finishing my pansy little cocktail and considering a replenishment when to my astonishment the entire Chinese family exited the igloo-shaped Tardis one by one, having changed into evening finery. They jumped into the BX19 and headed for the high spots of Brouville, as I stood there gawping.

Doctor Woo and his family were full of surprises, but not so full as the *Deutchebikerdykes* who arrived as the Chinese departed for their night of revelry.

Two identical BMW 800GS touring bikes growled to a halt and had their engines killed. The modern day knights of the road dismounted and commenced to peel off their armour. Gloves and helmets first, then layer after layer of thick, black, padded leather was removed to reveal layer after layer of flabby, white, unpadded cellulite, some of which struggled to be contained within over-stretched one piece swimming cozzies. The two eighteen stone wobbly masses became a single thirty-six stone wobbly mass as the *Deutchebikerdykes* embraced and commenced a five minute French kiss. 'When in Rome', and all that.

Kiss completed, the single mass became two masses once more and over-ample thighs were heartily slapped and wobbled as the first of many six-packs had their tops peeled off. It was well gone midnight when the by this time totally pissed masses became one again, in a huge double sleeping bag on the hard stony ground. No tent, no ground-sheet and presumably no pain, although there was a fair amount of groaning.

They had gone the next morning, evaporated, leaving only a big dent in the stony ground, a large amount of tissue paper and 28 crushed lager cans. Oh, and two empty yoghurt tubs, *fruhstuck*.

Martine arrived on her morning round, looked in blank amazement at the cans, the tissues and the dent and asked where the two German ladies on motor-bikes were.

"Gone," I said, "long before I got up. What are you going to do about the mess? All those cans and things?"

"I will get Jerome. He will tidy up. But they have not paid, they must pay."

"Forget it, ducks, they've long gone. Could be in Spain, Italy, Switzerland or back in their beloved Fatherland by now. Or should it be Motherland? Anyway, some you win!"

"*Quoi?*"

"Forget it."

She did, and Jerome forgot to tidy up as well. I did it, just in time.

The *Deutchebikerdykes* were immediately replaced by Smiling Svelte Sven and the Smorgesbord Kid, another two leather-clad knights of the road on two much racier machines, a Triumph Daytona and a Suzuki TC1000S, both single seat café-racer type of bikes. Scandinavian lads, as you will have gathered.

They quickly erected their 'stretch' version of the Chinese igloo, donned helmets and made off. It was mid afternoon when two delightful Dutch chicks arrived in an old Renault 5, parked next to the stretch igloo, got out and stood or sat around for ten minutes, smoking, as all Dutch do. Sven and the Kid burbled back on the bikes, dismounted and removed their helmets.

I was once again treated to five minutes of French kissing, heterosexual this time as the two lads took it in turns with the Cloggies. Swapping complete and appetites sated, the boys donned their helmets once more, jumped back on their bikes and burbled off, whilst the girls stripped off, pulled on the minutest of bikinis and headed for the beach.

Two quiet hours passed before I heard the distinctive exhaust notes again, this time followed by a taxi. Much one-sided chatter went on as two more chicks climbed out of the taxi, German I guessed, judging by the guttural expletives, and the driver tried to explain that any time the boys wanted a taxi just ring this number and himself or his wife would be only too pleased to ferry them and the lovely ladies wherever they wanted to go, day or night, time wasn't a problem, all they had to do was ring this number and either himself or his wife...

By this time Svelte Sven had stopped smiling, the Kid was half way down one chick's throat whilst the other one had a serious handful of his wedding tackle and Sven wanted in. The cabbie left and the two lads went at it hammer and tongs.

I really didn't know why they'd bothered erecting the tent, until the two Cloggies arrived back from the beach, just as Sven was coming up for breath and Doctor Woo and family pulled up in the battered Citroen. I was in tucks, it'd gone beyond a joke and from where I was trying to sit, blood-letting was on the cards. I ducked into the five-star accommodation and slid the curtain gently to one side.

Doctor Woo had put both hands over his teenage son's eyes, whilst his wife pulled their daughter hurriedly into the Tardis. It was too late, they'd already got an eyeful. The German girls had appraised the Dutch and vice versa.

The four girls, clearly deciding that whatever was contained within the Scandinavian biking leathers was superfluous to requirements and that a bit of versa vice was in order, all dived into the stretch igloo. The *Deutchebikerdykedent* had left more than just a physical impression, it seemed.

Sven and the Kid shrugged at each other, pulled on their helmets, mounted up and burbled off once again. It was all too much for the ageing Vice Big Knob of the WANCAs (a country member). I simply couldn't take any more. *Pastis* was required. I reached the Volvo on hands and knees, this state caused partly by mirth, partly confusion and partly embarrassment. Not equal measures, but damned nearly. I made it to the Café unscathed, did the telephone watch and returned to what I'd hoped would be a nice, quiet, tidy scene, the sort more becoming of Le Camping Municipal, Brouville.

No bloody chance!

The bikes were back and in my parking space was a VW Golf and loud giggles and moans were emanating from the stretch igloo. More Dutch chicks. Smiling Svelte Sven and the Smorgesbord Kid were positively awesome.

I used to have a pal in London when I worked there in the mid-sixties, Rod was his name and a damned appropriate one. His only chat up line was 'Do you want a fuck?' He had a remarkable amount of success did Rod. It was, I suppose, the scatter-gun approach. He wasn't too fussy what kind of young lady was on the end of this apposite line, or his rod for that matter. I reckoned that the Scandinavian lads were working on a similar approach and earmarked them for a drink the next day. Just sitting on the doorstep waiting for cast-offs could prove to be more lucrative than everything I'd got to offer.

Holiday Camp Fever was beginning to bite!

Unlike Butlin's, Le Camping didn't have nightly entertainment, no glittering third-rate showbiz affairs hosted by Red Coats. You see, I do know something about Butlin's. I'll tell you how.

Some years ago I was involved in the organisation of a sales conference for a client of the advertising agency where I occupied desk space at the time. The theme of this conference was 'Changes', the client company trying desperately to drag their stick-in-the-mud sales force into the twentieth century. I spent some time with the chap who was to be MC and anchorman for the conference and we devised what we thought was a jolly good way of getting the theme over. I made three short video programmes using a mixture of stills and library footage, all along the lines of how some things change and others don't. After the videos had been shown, the MC would invite the sales force to pick an image from the programme and that would trigger discussion. He gave me a comprehensive list of suitable images to choose from, one of which was 'holiday camps'. I paid a visit to a travel agent, picked up a Butlin's brochure and chose the image of the glittering entertainment to portray in the video.

On the day, one salesman picked this image and I flashed the still up on the huge back projection screen. Discussion commenced, but not before the MC explained to his captive audience that whilst we'd been putting the programmes together he'd remarked to me that the image I had chosen so evocatively portrayed the holiday camp of the Fifties and where had I found the photo. I'd told him, from that year's Butlin's brochure.

Marylin Pat was the closest Le Camping Municipal could come to a regular Red Coat. She appeared each week on a Wednesday night, set up her sophisticated karaoke machine at Le Cab and warbled the night away. There's no denying she was well worth looking at and her voice was half way decent, but her pronunciation of the English lyrics in some of the better known songs brought a smile to the English faces watching and she had all the charisma of a house brick, ending each song with:

"Merci. Alors, j'continue avec..." and then the title of the song she was going to *continue avec.*

Just that, song after song after song, and her Seventies disco girl movements, standing on one spot just moving her ankles from side to side, didn't create too much atmosphere either, but it was live, well liveish, entertainment and the best you could expect at Le Camping Municipal, Brouville.

The Karaoke man who put in an occasional appearance did manage to get one or two people onto the stage, mostly a rather plump young girl who mucked out the horses at the Riding School next door. Again, she had a good voice and even dueted with Marylin Pat on a couple of occasions, but the svelte songstress was never under any serious threat of competition, in either the looks or charisma departments.

For most of the month of July and the first week in August, I had a French family staying at two permanent caravans on a pitch next door but one, a grandfather and grandmother, their daughter and grand-daughter. As well as the two caravans they also had a campervan, a huge and capacious affair which could have easily accommodated the four of them and in which it must have been possible for days to pass without seeing each other. However, they chose the two caravans in which to spend their summer holidays. The evening, night and early morning part of their holidays, that is. At 9.30 each day, the family ensemble would form a crocodile behind grandfather and shuffle to the campervan, climb in and sit solemnly waiting whilst grandfather started the engine, waited for it to warm up and move off. They would then drive to a car park on the lakeside half way between the campsite and the village, park under a huge tree and mooch about until five o'clock. Every day, as regular as Mr Goodbody's wall and Luke's dump.

The day this family had arrived was a notable one.

It was a few days after my electricity had been connected, via a cable which ran overhead through the trees. I'd arrived back at Le Camping after a good afternoon's yott and was chased to my parking spot by the totally bald, bull-headed grandfather, Jacques, who'd introduced himself and apologised. I couldn't work out what the hell he was apologising for until he dragged me out of the Volvo and over to a tree, where he showed me the limp bare end of my electricity cable dangling from the branches above. Transpires the campervan had ripped it to shreds as he'd driven up.

In the interests of neighbourliness, I went to the Volvo and returned to the tree with my comprehensive tool kit. Jacques wrenched it away from me and did a solid repair job on the cable. We decided it would be judicious to let this section of my power supply run along the ground, at least for the duration of their holiday, during the duration of which I was to observe weirder and weirder behaviour from this strange family.

Jacques had a nasty habit of creeping up behind me and slapping me hard on the back with a whoop. He nearly caused several heart attacks with this trick and adding to my palpitations was the sight of grand-daughter, perhaps eleven or twelve years old, crouching in the middle of a ring of smaller children which she'd gathered round her in the trees. Head and arms thrown back, she was baying like a wolf as the other children, eyes like saucers, mimicked her.

At no time did anything resembling a husband/father turn up. I had thought perhaps that the daughter's hubby may be working and might join the family for a week or two, or a long weekend maybe. But no, nobody did and such was the womenfolk's demeanour, drooping shoulders, sour, dull faces as long as a wet fortnight, that I did start to wonder.

The power which Jacques wielded over the females was daunting, the grand-daughter so obviously terrified of him that she was oft seen scurrying into the trees and crouching there for long periods of time with a look of abject terror on her face. The daughter, her mother, took not a blind bit of notice and wordlessly went about her chores. Grandmother had a curious look on her face most of the time, I couldn't work out whether it was a grin or a grimace, but it sure as hell was curious. Every time Jacques shouted something at her the corners of the ugly, mis-formed mouth curled up, long, blackened teeth were fully exposed to daylight and it became more of a grin, but no word issued forth.

I was starting to invent dark and bizarre theories about this lot, so convinced was I that the grand-daughter was two sandwiches short of a picnic and her mother not much brighter. Whenever they saw me, they were all cheerful and friendly, waving and smiling, '*Allo*, Peetair', '*Bonjour*, Peetair' and all that sort of stuff, but I found myself scampering for cover in the caravan as five o'clock drew nigh and I heard the sound of the campervan approaching. I bravely cowered until they had passed by.

They're probably the most charming and delightful, close-knit and loving family you're ever likely to meet, and to cap it all, a couple of days after I'd written the bulk of this part of the tale, I felt a slap on my shoulder but no whoop, and turned to find Jacques holding his right hand out for me to shake whilst thrusting a bottle of *Bretonne Cidre* at me with the left.

They were leaving, he said, and wanted to wish me luck. I hope they never get to read this tale.

Chapter 11

GREY CLOUDS, SILVER LININGS

*In which I tell of the one and only rainstorm
of the summer, more attempts at official
chartering and the pedalo people.*

Martine had said it would rain in August. In the afternoons, or early evenings. It always did, she added. She wasn't wrong, about the rain, the timing was a bit off.

On August 1st we had a couple of afternoon showers, just showers, not enough time to pull on a waterproof jacket or run for cover. Quick bursts and then it stopped and the sun came out again. That evening I wrote a postcard gleefully to this effect. I knew that England was experiencing considerable rainfall from my telephone calls to Mother, Luke and Beth, and just wanted to make my pals back home jealous. I went to *La Poste* late the next morning, bought a stamp, stuck it on the postcard and popped it through the postbox slot, the one with a Union Jack on. I was smiling.

Then suddenly the sky went dark, very, very dark and very, very suddenly everything above me was just one great big cloud, gunmetal grey and threatening.

As I hurried towards the Volvo, remembering that the sun-roof was open, my hat and shoulders were bombarded with solid lumps of water. It wasn't rain, not the sort of rain you get in England. It was a machine gun attack, it hurt like hell and didn't stop for nigh on two days.

My world was transformed, the sun-kissed world, the one to which I'd accustomed myself these past two months. I made it back to the car, soaked to the skin and sitting on an equally soaking seat, closed the sun-roof and started back to Le Camping, a slow, tedious journey, undertaken in a state of blind hysteria.

Blind, because the great big lumps of water hit the bonnet and bounced so far into the air before returning for another go it rendered the windscreen wipers totally useless. Hysteria set in as

I quickly realised that everybody else had the same idea — head for the safety of your home, permanent or temporary, we were under attack. Brouville's promenade was transformed into a huge dodgem rink, the surface of which resembled that of Le Lac. Above the deafening roar of the machine gun attack I could distinctly hear the sound of crumpling metal and tinkling glass as car after car bounced and crunched its way to safety. Nobody hit the Volvo and it didn't hit anybody — we made it back to the caravan unscathed and I pulled to a halt on the solid piece of hard-standing right next to the caravan door.

Key at the ready, I tore open the car door and stepped out, and down. The sun-baked earth which had hitherto provided me with a solid parking space had been transformed into a large patch of soft, gooey brown stuff and I sank into it, almost up to my knees. It was like quicksand, and having made the relative safety of the plank which represented my door-step, pulling each foot out of the quicksand with great difficulty and superhuman strength, I turned to watch as the Volvo sank slowly up to its axles, the hot exhaust hissing its disapproval. My deck shoes were down there somewhere as well.

As I turned the key and let myself into the caravan a thought darker than the sky itself crossed my mind. I had no sustenance, except an unfinished bottle of red wine, my marmalade, one tin of sardines and a small jar of olives, and no way of replenishing stocks. The car was firmly stuck, and I'd transferred my waterproofs and wellies to the boat some while before. I was stranded.

I towelled off, changed into dry clothes and pulled my walking boots and shower-proof jacket on, the one item of vaguely wet weather gear I'd kept in the caravan, but it was only shower-proof, not bullet-proof.

It was a despondent trudge to Le Cabanon and an even more despondent Marsh who, minutes later, was knocking on Martine's door. Le Cab had put up the shutters and the Stefs had locked themselves in, presumably to each others' arms. They weren't going to get any customers for the rest of that day.

Martine was near to collapsing with laughter as I described my predicament, but insisted that I remove my soaking wet clothes and she provided me with a towel and her bath robe. I dried off for the second time in fifteen minutes and sat at the table, shivering in the tiny robe. I'm not a big person but Martine is half my size and the robe and towel combined to only just save my modesty and her blushes.

I pulled my tobacco tin out of the wet jeans' pocket as Martine went over to the cooker and started to prepare a pasta bake. At least she'd not let me starve, but the little French thing is very anti-smoking. When we'd been out sailing one day she'd spotted a fire, high up a hillside, next to a road. The Pumped-up Ones had soon brought it under control, but Martine shouted angrily, to nobody in particular,

"Bloody smokers, flicking the cigarette into the bush."

I'd said nothing, just grinned and lit up.

"No! Not in here, please!"

She'd turned and saw what I was doing but her words were superfluous. The tobacco was a sodden brown ball and the packet of Rizlas resembled a soggy, cardboard loo-roll dispenser, the 'finest quality gummed papers' transformed into one continuous sheet.

The pasta was soon done and I enjoyed an afternoon's nicotine-free conversation.

Martine explained a lot about the French way of doing things, official things that is. The subject had inevitably come around to my chartering and I told her what I'd started doing whilst she had been away on holiday. She'd nodded sagely and agreed that it was the best I could do and she would mention it to the incoming English or English-speaking campers — unofficially. Thereafter we had quite a good and relatively safe system. Martine would fix up my charters and I would go alone to the pontoon, motoring or more often sailing over to the campsite beach to pick up and later drop off my fares. This kept my activities very low-key and had the added advantage of allowing me to say that these folk were my acquaintances, friends from Le Camping.

Since Napoleonic times, France has been a solid socialist state, despite the elections held the previous March at which the right-wing National Front had achieved sweeping success in the south of the country. As such, self-employment is still frowned upon and even the French themselves find many stumbling blocks in their way, put there presumably to make it as difficult as possible and therefore an unwelcome avenue for folk to take.

For a start there are the tax laws, always assuming you have managed to get through the quagmire of registering for business, paying handsomely for that privilege and getting your *Assurances* in order. An individual has to estimate how much he is going to earn in the first twelve month period and start paying tax immediately he starts trading. The plus or minus is then worked out at the end of that period. This applies to income tax, local taxes and *TVA* (VAT), which has to be paid monthly. And it is the *Maire* who must ensure that everybody trading in his *Commune* is not only registered to trade but is paying their taxes. The casual trader such as myself, despite having mayoral approval, has to toe the line and to do so would have cost me more than I'd earn in the first season. It's easy to see how I'd incurred the jealousy of the other folk trading in the seasonal tourist business, all French, and doing their trade under these stringent laws. For me to come along and blatantly wave my red duster in their faces, claiming that I was not only sailing under the British flag but trading under British tax laws, would surely see me facing an unofficial guillotine, before the official one was pressed into service.

So that afternoon, whilst I chatted away and enjoyed Martine's pasta bake, the rain was well and truly falling from the grey clouds, physically as well as metaphorically. I suppose I had hoped that I could find a way of doing my business, and I suppose you could say I did, but it was totally illegal and a tad on the nerve-wracking side.

The lightning lit up the stark campsite which had taken on a look of Stalag Luft 3 after curfew.

Where just that morning the happy little Dutch, German, French and Belgian children had been at play, the ground on which they had done their playing now resembled yet another tributary of

171

the mighty River Durance. I splashed along, ankle deep in rushing water as overhead the thunder roared, rolling all around the neighbouring mountains and threatening to burst my eardrums.

It was no better inside the caravan. The once dry air now had a distinctly damp feel, wet even and, when I went for yet another change of clothes, I was reminded of a yacht delivery I'd done some years ago when stuck in a rain-lashed, gale Force 8 Atlantic for ten days. Everything was damp and no way of airing it. Even the sleeping bag was wet, the atmosphere so heavily laden with humidity.

I tried to read for a while but the light flickered every time the lightning flashed so, fearing that my one and only bulb might burst, I turned it off and tried my best to find sleep.

The next day passed slowly, very slowly, and very noisily as the unrelenting machine gun attack continued to make dints in the caravan roof, which fortunately withstood the attack and steadfastly refused to leak.

Martine had let me have a packet of those toast-shaped cracker things, so I had some padding to take with my marmalade, olives and sardines. I remembered having boiled up a flask full of water aboard Rip-Rap the day before and it was still in the Volvo. I made a sodden dash to retrieve it and thankfully the water was still warm, warm enough for two or three cups of instant coffee. The unfinished wine was finished and a considerable number of book pages were read.

And that, so to speak, was August 3rd, 1998.

August 4th, 1998 will stand by its predecessor in stark comparison.

The first thing I noticed was the silence — one of those silences which novelists refer to as being 'deafening', whatever the hell that means. Silence is silence, it's quiet, there is no noise and that is why it is called 'silence', and that is what I woke up to, nothing. No noise, just silence.

I peered out of my still damp sleeping bag at the curtain above my head. It was blindingly bright, or at least the light coming through it was. Here we go again, I thought, Provence is back to normal. Whoever instigated the machine gun attack had now capitulated and moved on to pastures new, hopefully Thailand or somewhere equally distant. I struggled out of the damp and into the dry, and then the silence did become deafening.

The first of six twin-engined seaplanes skimmed just feet above the trees and dipped down towards the lake, the screaming aero engines shook the still-sodden ground and left my ear drums tingling.

The yellow and red planes, with *'Securité Civile'* emblazoned along their fuselages, were here to collect water from Le Lac; there was a fire that needed putting out and obviously a pretty damn big one, too big for your average Pumped-up Soppy Ones. Odd, after all that rain, I thought, but pulled on my last remaining set of dampish-dry clothes and headed through the trees and down towards the beach in order to get a view of the air/water-borne operation.

It's awesome — the planes touch down almost in line ahead on the surface of the lake, scoot along for a couple of hundred yards or so, kicking up one hell of a spray whilst sucking up hundreds of gallons of water each, then lumber gently back into the air, banking steeply and turning back in the general direction of the fire, which was destined to have their loads dumped on it. I cursed for not remembering my camera and then thanked somebody up there that I wasn't trying to tack in or out of the lagoon at the time. It'd have been reminiscent of Pearl Harbour, no warning sirens, just a very long silence preceded by a loud deafening, as wave after wave of planes came straight at Rip-Rap and me, their pilots screaming whatever 'Tora, Tora, Tora' is in French.

I watched as Les Kamikazes wheeled away and spotted their destination. A huge cloud of thick, grey smoke rose lazily up from behind the bare mountain range which marks the eastern end of the largest military camp in Europe, I'm told. Clearly the gun-toting ones had been having an illegal Bar-B-Q (my theory), or maybe one of them had just inadvertently flicked his fag-end into a bush (Martine's theory).

The rest of August 4th passed with considerably less excitement. Although fine and dry, there were still a few clouds around and the sun was taking its time to re-heat Brouville.

As I climbed back through the woods towards the campsite I saw a group of mainly Dutch folk heaving and groaning against the back of Jacques' campervan. It was parked next to the Volvo and equally stuck. I ran over to add my eleven stone to the effort and eventually there was a loud 'plop' as the van tyres extricated themselves from the gooey stuff. Jacques jumped out and pumped everybody's hands in turn, then turned to the Volvo and told them all to do the same for me. Brilliant. Out she came and after a more subdued thank-you ceremony, I popped down to the village. Supplies needed to be laid in against another machine gun attack and I also required a *Télécarte*.

All French phone boxes seem to be card operated, no coin boxes for Les Hooligans to raid, and my previous card had run out. *'Télécarte'* is one of the most difficult French words to enunciate, for me anyway, or so it would seem. No matter how I say it I am always met with a blank stare, sometimes accompanied by a *'Quoi?'*. Latterly I'd tried adding *'pour le téléphone'* to my attempted pronunciation, but all that did was add a *'pour le téléphone?'* to the *'Quoi?'*.

"Of course it's for *le* fucking *téléphone*, you simple Gallic moron!" I'd ventured on one occasion, with a smile.

All that did was extract another *'Quoi?'*, so I'd given up.

The only person who understood what I wanted was the nice young *mademoiselle* at La Poste in Brouville. After all, I only went there for *'Timbres'* or *'Télécartes'* and you don't have to have a First Class Honours degree to work out it's one or t'other. The only problem I had with *mam'selle* was getting across the denomination of the *Télécarte* I required, 10 units, 25 units or 50 units. August 4th was the big one's turn, I had quite a few calls to make.

"*Le grand!*" I replied emphatically in response to her question, which I understood by inference alone.

She peeled one off and I slipped a hundred *franc* note into the coin tray. It was only when I was leaving that I checked my change and immediately turned back to the counter.

"Come on, dearie. *Un* 50 *franc* note, *s'il vous plait*," I hissed angrily through clenched teeth and the bullet-proof glass.

She looked frightened and made a big flustering fuss and demanded to see my newly acquired *Télécarte*.

"*Oui, Oui,*" she said, pointing feverishly at the silver piece of plastic in my hand. "*Oui.*"

I looked carefully at it and blushed. Well I didn't know they had 120 unit ones, did I? Armed with my silver flexible friend, the card-key to long, lascivious chats with Beth and ultimately short, gut-wrenching ones with my solicitor, I turned in to the Café du Soleil.

For days before, François had worn the expression of a worried man, and many reasons had been crossing my mind.

One early morning I'd caught him sitting alone in the deserted terrace restaurant slowly going through invoicey looking papers and shaking his head. Ahh, money worries, I'd thought. Surely not, the season had started and folk were flocking to pay the best part of ten quid for a bit of lettuce, a couple of olives, the odd anchovy and a slice or two of egg and tomato. Then he'd taken to barking at the staff, upsetting all of them and creating such a bad atmosphere that I'd started to avoid the place. Staff problems? Never. They were honed to perfection, Sergeant Milko keeping them finely balanced on toes of silk, balletic in their movements and quality of service. Then I was to get a bit of a shock.

I'd turned in as François was turning out, his car ticking over impatiently on the road outside.

"Peetair, I am going. I'm so sorry".

Jesus, he's going to top himself! And what had I done to force him into this course of action? Was it that I'd been avoiding the place? Was he angry that the chartering business wasn't bringing any extra custom? Why tell me he was sorry?

"I have to go to see my children, and... my wife."

The saddest hang-dog face hung sadly to one side.

"Katrine! She's left you?"

I couldn't believe it. It seemed only days before that we'd had a chat and I'd told her that Beth would be coming to see me soon and how much Katrine said she looked forward to meeting her.

"Yes. And now I must go and see... see what can be done. We are all human you know, even my wife."

I wasn't too sure how to reply to that one, so I didn't. I just put my hand on his shoulder, squeezed it and wished him luck.

Then I settled into a chair and a *pastis* and thought thoughts of how precarious every damned little thing in this life of ours is.

I'd settled into one too many *pastis* and was settling the bill a little while later when one of the least precarious things in life shuffled up.

"Allo everybodee!"

Here we go again. I did the handshake routine, got my wallet out, ordered liquid aniseedy things and commenced banter.

It'd been a while since I'd seen the buck-toothed Croat and during the course of the conversation Bruno told me that there was a film crew in the area and he'd had a request to provide a boat from which they could do some filming on the lake and would I like to do it? At least that's what I thought he'd said.

I could barely contain my excitement, big bucks film crew and Rip-Rap at the ready and it was bound to be 'readies', I know a bit about the film side of things. The excitement grew until his English-speaking wife Jo turned up a little while later and explained to me that the film crew had been there the previous week and try though he might Bruno couldn't find me and just had to do the job himself. Bugger, bugger, bugger.

Silver cloud, grey lining.

August 4th, 1998 ended, for me anyway, on yet another low note.

Eleven o'clock, on the morning of August 5th found me sitting once more outside the Café, this time with *une grande tasse de* coffee in front of me. It was required.

I'd spoken to the Big Knob briefly that morning and asked him to ring me at the Café when he got to work, as he'd returned from his holliers and I just knew there'd be a yarn or two. The telephone shrilled and Milko came out with the portable handset.

"Garree. *Pour vous*," he said.

I tell you, that lad's missing his way. He'd make a mighty fine butler, but on second thoughts he probably wouldn't meet too many female Dutch holidaymakers being a gentleman's gentleman.

I wasn't wrong about Gazzer's holiday, almost a yarn too far.

You may recall that he'd sold Hunca Munca and bought a sister ship to Big Dave's Trenarth, a Nicholson 31 called 'Picnic' (where do we get these names from?). She was based in Antwerp and Gaz had taken Dunc and another pal of his to help fetch her across the Channel. They had a great three days getting as far as Dover, the others returned to work and womenfolk and Gaz set off to get Picnic as close to the Straits as was possible in what remained of his fortnight's holiday. Milford Haven is the quick answer, but one or two of the yarns he told me will give you a flavour of the trip.

Waving a tearful farewell to his shipmates, Gaz weaved out of Dover harbour dodging the ferries, hovercraft, jetfoils and other assorted water-borne grockle carriers, then turned west for Brighton. Half way there the wind dropped, it was straight on the nose anyway, so the donkey was brought to life, but it wouldn't propel the boat along. The propeller was jammed.

Gaz headed back for Dover, running before what wind there was and radioed in to the Harbourmaster with his problem. You are not allowed to sail into Dover, such is the confusion of craft at that time of the year, so they told Gaz to wait outside and then sent a huge powerful launch to tow him in and they dumped him against the harbour wall.

Our hero was too ashamed to tell anybody that it was his jib sheet he'd got wrapped around the prop — he'd found that out when trying to get the headsail back into the roller-reefing. So into the oily waters of Dover harbour went our man and cut the offending bit of string away from the prop.

He set off once more and a few other minor adventures later found our intrepid denizen in Helford River, head into a Force 7 when the jib halyard broke and the headsail tumbled to the deck. He threw down the hook and struggled manfully for the next three quarters of an hour to get the massive genoa down below.

Succeeding eventually, he then noticed that he'd dragged

anchor and was a mere fifty feet from some very jagged and unforgiving looking rocks. The donkey was fired up, started first time and just as quickly stopped. And again, and again. It's difficult enough to sail off anchor with just the mainsail in the best of conditions, especially when you're single-handed, but wind against a very close and jagged shore on a falling tide is not the place to try it, especially as the wind was in the region of 40 knots and you're in a strange boat with an intermittently non-functioning engine.

A quick call to the Coastguards, just to let them know he was up Helford Creek without a certain instrument, and Gaz rummaged for his spare anchor, which was of course at the bottom of the locker with all manner of unnecessary crap on top of it. Just in time the hook was attached and deposited over the side, fortunately gripping instantly and avoiding certain bankruptcy. Gaz has always erred on the side of the cheapskate when it comes to insuring things.

He finished off our conversation by telling me that Big Dave, The Swimmer and Rear Big Knob of the WANCAs had had a 'heart do' whilst aboard Trenarth on his own. It was early one morning and the poor old bugger had to get into his dinghy and row over to the nearest boat and bang on the hull. The owner, a policeman, was fortunately aboard and soon had Dave whisked into hospital where he was recovering.

"S'pose there's an up-side to all this," said Gaz, cheerfully. "He'll perhaps get early retirement now."

I'd just finished my chat with Gaz and returned the handset to its self-charging cradle on the Café bar, when François hove into sight, with a grin on his face. I asked him how things were and he shrugged, continued to smile and said,

"I think it will be all right... I think."

A few uneventful days later I was sitting on Le Bouchon bar terrace when Milko plonked himself down next to me.

There was absolutely no wind whatsoever and I'd wanted a sail. It was hot and humid and sitting in the cockpit of Rip-Rap enjoying a beer and a cooling breeze was most appealing, but not to be. The next best thing would be a beer and a bout of banter with a pal or two, and here was an opportunity for such, but with rather an unusual sparring partner considering it was the middle of the afternoon and Milko should've been on duty at the Café.

He'd left, he said, *'terminée'*, finished.

François' mood-swings had got to him and he'd slung his hook. We chatted on for ten minutes or so, mainly about François and his sorry marital plight, when suddenly I felt a breeze. It wasn't from the usual direction, this one was coming from exactly opposite to where the Mistral comes from. Milko gave it its name, *'Vent de l'Est'*, and I jumped to my feet.

"You get some supplies, Milko," I said, handing him a 100 *franc* note. "We're going sailing."

I legged it down to the pontoon as Milko headed off for the shops, de-rigged everything and prepared Rip-Rap for a yott. My shipmate arrived, laden with all manner of goodies and we cast-off, heading out of the lagoon with a Force 4 up our chuff. The stiff breeze was giving us six plus knots and we barely had time to wave to the Café as Rip-Rap powered out into the middle of the lake.

We made it over to my favourite lagoon, which was sheltered from this strange wind, and threw down the hook. There we passed a lazy afternoon.

Milko's idea of supplies were consumed with gusto — *poulet, saucisson, pâté, tomate, camembert,* you name it, all plastered onto *baguettes* and washed down with Eurofizz, which was still ice cold having been stowed in the cool-box.

He's a man of many faces is Milko, and names.

Patric is his real one (his father had nicknamed him Milko because of his nearly white blonde hair) and he was born and brought up in Algeria, where his father held a diplomatic post of some description. He'd turned to waiting, mainly because he wanted to be an actor, but Dad wouldn't let him. It was the next best thing, he figured and he does put on a good act. Despite being temporarily out of work, I was certain it wouldn't be long before any of the other eateries in Brouville took him on and then there was always the winter job in the Alps awaiting him.

We pulled up the hook around seven o'clock and headed back to Brouville. It was a tough beat into the lagoon and a weary Marsh who finally arrived back at Le Camping around nine.

I pulled up outside Martine's place and was heading for Le Cab when she saw me and came out for a chat. I persuaded her to join me and we passed a pleasant hour before she headed off for the sack. She had to be up at six to muck out the toilet block. It's not all beer and skittles being a campsite receptionist.

I showered and changed and headed back to Le Cab for a nightcap. It was quiet, only Stef and his two waiters, sitting at a table and nattering, the female Steph being absent, and a gang of five girls who were doing a lot of secretive giggling as they consumed copious ales. Then the bovine Bretons arrived.

My first week at the campsite had been very quiet indeed, only Martine, Stefan and myself being resident there, and the Breton.

In France, the Bretons are likened to the Irish in England and all manner of jokes are told about them, mostly the same ones we tell about the Guinness-guzzling, potato-munching Paddies. This particular Breton had a pedalo business which rivaled that of Sylvan Arnoux and I had toyed with the idea of approaching him with my chartering plan when Son of the Dark One had declined my offer. I took an instant dislike to the fellow. He was rude, uncouth, smelly and thick and he had bad teeth, so I didn't bother. He didn't fit the front-man image I had in mind for my up-market charters.

Gradually, as the summer wore on and more and more tourists arrived, so did members of the Breton's family. Two more bovine brothers came, with their wives and children, all bearing a remarkable resemblance to François' *entrecôte* on the hoof, and equally rude, uncouth, smelly and thick.

That night they barged into Le Cab *en masse* and proceeded to re-arrange the tables and chairs to their liking, knocking over my *pastis* and laughing in the process. Stef saw this and re-charged my glass apologetically. Then he pulled the girls' table up to theirs and the Bretons', whilst one of the waiters started filling litre *carafes* with *rosé* wine. It was going to be a party and clearly I wasn't invited.

I stoicly sat my ground and sipped on, internally seething yet determined to finish my drink in my own time, whilst in reality I would have rather been elsewhere, any bloody where.

I was forced to listen to the conversation (you could've heard it on the beach) which centred around one of the girls, who was celebrating her eighteenth birthday, an occasion which had inadvertently brought about this impromptu rave and which I can assure you wouldn't have happened had the female Steph been in attendance.

Le Cab's CD player was pressed into service as more *rosé* was poured, all on the house, and the bovine Breton seized his opportunity to rival Stefan's gesture with the wine by offering the girls a free hour on a pedalo the next day. There was much mirth and back-slapping at this blatant show of generosity, a quality for which the Bretons are not highly noted, being akin to the Scots in this department. I'd had enough, it was time to turn in.

A grey cloud had appeared over what had until fifteen minutes before been a lovely day, so curbing an over-whelming desire to throw up, I stood up, bade farewell to Stef and made off.

Then something happened, a blinding flash exploded somewhere in my head. An overpowering sensation, I can't help or explain it. The flash repeated, twice, three times, and the Marsh trait of making mirth, shit-stirring and general evilry welled up as I paused at the girl's end of the table.

"Happy birthday," I said to the young lady whose party it had become. "Do you speak English?"

"Yes, of course. And thank you."

Her eyes twinkled, the smile was stunning. A couple more flashes.

"In that case, how about having a real treat tomorrow, as a birthday gift from an Englishman abroad." I paused, for theatrical effect. Another flash. "You must all come and enjoy a day sailing on my yacht."

It was irresistible. Once more, I'd lit the blue touch paper and chucked a rip-rap in the general direction of girls' legs. They squealed, this time with delight.

"You have a yacht?" one of the others exclaimed, breathlessly.

"Yes. She's moored on the pontoon at Brouville and called Rip-Rap. I'll see you all about twelve, OK? You can have your *aperitif* on the piddling plastic pedalo," I glanced at the Breton, "and then come for a real feast of proper yottin'. How's that?"

Kerrumph!!

A star-burst rocket exploded in the midnight blue sky above me, as I walked away from the silent gathering of bovine ones. Behind me, the girlish giggling became so infectious that I was forced to smile.

Then silver stardust sprinkled all around.

Chapter 12

TOUJOURS ENGLAND

In which I tell of a gang of ex-pats abroad
and Mother's visit.

Mother's arrival in Provence heralded yet another chapter, a slice of Provençal life hitherto denied to yours truly.

It all came about because François introduced me to Chris. This was four or five days before Mother was due to arrive and I had done an early-twirly bird, disappearing up my own bum. Quite what the hell I was going to do with the 82 year old, I'd not a clue. Yes, she wanted to go to Pruniers and Seyne and Tourtour — she'd been to these places on her painting holiday some years before and had mentioned the fact. She was, however, supposed to be with Beth and that would have softened the blow, but for various reasons, Beth couldn't come. Now I was facing six days with the senile delinquent and not a clue how to entertain her.

Sitting glumly at the Café one evening and mulling over ideas, François stepped over with his arm around the shoulders of a rather acceptable looking chap and informed me that this was Chris. We shook hands and I invited him to join me. An hour or so passed, during which time much banter took place and the odd drink was thrown down. We parted the best of mates and I'd been invited to join an elite circle of ex-pats at a bar in Seyne the following Wednesday, the day before the impending arrival of the aged one.

"Can I introduce Peter, everybody. Pete, this is Leo, Christiana, Felix, my wife Wendy, Stuart, Penny, Hamish..." it went on and on. There were at least a dozen and, as time went by, more joined in.

Initially, I was sandwiched between Leo and Felix, Dutch and Belgian respectively, but both speaking perfect English. The conversation always took place in English, I was informed, and this day switched from world politics to why Belgian number plates are always old and rusty, how and why I should visit Amsterdam in August and why Belgians never laugh, but it was never dull. English-speaking banter had returned to my life.

The whole gathering seemed to be orchestrated by Chris, who would leap to somebody's side and drag them into conversation when it looked as if things were flagging. An hour or more passed, whilst not only Chris, but others as well, joined in the musical chairs. The best bit I can remember was staring into Christiana's eyes, they reminded me of Beth's, but Christiana is married to Felix. And then Chris announced the *pièce de résistance*. Lunch.

The majority of the gang, there were one or two gibbers, walked across the road to La Provençale, a restaurant I had looked at on a number of occasions, but written off as being too expensive. Chris had his arm around me and so I had no alternative, did I?

A table was arranged to accommodate our party and the menus were given out. I couldn't believe what I was seeing — a full three course lunch for 59FF (£5.90), including a small *carafe* of wine per person. Hitherto I must have only looked at the *à la carte* menu on display outside, this little gem had escaped me. A choice of two starters, two main courses and a wide variety of desserts. I ordered the *pâté* to start, a portion at least 6 by 4 inches and half an inch thick, well done steak and *pommes frites* with side salad and a huge dollop of pistachio ice cream.

The afternoon passed in the warmest of *bonhomie*, the warmest of the sun being shaded by vines and the bill arrived. Much extra wine had been ordered and served and drunk, the *carafes* getting larger each time, but I didn't care. Six quid and a pound or two more for the extra wine. What the hell. This was living. I had at last found a reason for believing that this was why I was here in Provence and that Peter Mayle had been right, damn him!

Hamish collected the money, he always does, apparently. Twelve people all stuffed to the gunwales, one or two of us just a tad tipsy, and we got change from £100! I left the restaurant as I'd entered, Chris and I arm in arm.

"Will you come on Saturday, Pete? We do this every Wednesday and Saturday, market days."

"Well... I'm not sure, Chris. I've got Mother coming out for a week and... well..."
"Brilliant! Bring her along. That's brilliant."
And it was.

"The last time I was here, in Seyne, we stayed at a little café just down past the *pharmacie*. I've been to look for it but it's a poodle parlour now."
Mother, as always, was holding the floor.
I had taken her to Seyne to meet the gang and she immediately fell in with the older girls, Yvonne, Veronica and Josephine, (Vonny, Ronny and Joss). They'd huddled hilariously for an hour and now we were in La Prov having the customary lunch and Mother was regaling the entire company with the story of her painting holiday which was mighty funny when I first heard it, but wears a bit thin on the two hundred and ninety third telling. The gang were in tucks, so much so that it even brought a smile to my face. I couldn't have hoped for a better environment in which to dump the old thing.
"At last!" exclaimed Hamish. "We've met a client of the place."
Transpires that the cafè Mother had stayed at had only lasted a few weeks before going bankrupt and the gang were intensely interested to find out the inside story. It's a very close knit community, the ex-pats in Seyne, and they must find out exactly what's going on. Past, present and future.
After Mother's tale had drawn to its inevitable climax and the gang clutched stomachs and tears rolled down cheeks, Chris, the first to recover, announced that they were all going to a *Brocante* in Villecroze the following day and we simply must join them. This could get no better. The six days would whiz by in a flash and I'd soon be dropping the old girl off at Nice airport.

"What in God's name does that do?"
"Your guess, old chap, is as good as mine."
Chris and I were gazing at the most peculiar copper object, a sort of oval tank perhaps 18 inches high by 10 across, with some extraordinary tubes, levers and twiddly things on it. There was

also a gauze filter of some description on the top. Being an engineer, I thought Chris might have a clue to the object's use, but no. He was as baffled as I.

We were at the *Brocante*, a kind of French car boot sale, but all over the streets and square, and not a boot in sight, except a pair of very old ones, well past their walk-by date and extremely expensive. They must have had a sentimental value to the chap selling them, or an historic one. Perhaps they'd belonged to Gendarme Gevaudan de Nantes, who has a monument or two in his memory and even a street named after him in Seyne. I've asked around for the story of Gendarme Gevaudan, he must have been quite a chap, but nobody can shed any light on the fellow's fame. I intend to pursue my research into the noble *flic's* past so if these were his boots, I might have been tempted to stump up the 250FF. I enquired, but the vendor just shrugged his shoulders and grimaced. I walked on, feeling 25 quid better off.

Mother was sitting at a bar table with Wendy, Chris's wife and they were deep in earnest conversation when Chris and I wandered up and ordered ale. We hadn't bought anything, but Penny had.

Penny is Hamish's partner and they have a remarkable relationship, both pursuing careers which take them to the four corners of the globe and meeting up occasionally at their villa just outside Seyne. This week was one of those occasions.

Penny had bought an extremely ugly jug for 30FF. It was the object of much scorn and derision, as the gathering at the bar moved on to a restaurant which Chris had had the foresight to book the previous day. The Villecroze *Brocante* is seemingly very popular and restaurant seats are as hen's teeth on the day.

The gang gathered round and commenced eating, whilst much mirth was made, particularly in the direction of Penny's jug. After only pecking at her *Salade Nicoise* for ten minutes, Penny picked up her jug and made to leave.

I don't think it was the derision, Penny can hold her own with the best of them, she said it was jet-lag. She'd only returned from a white water rafting expedition on the Zambesi the previous morning and announced she was feeling sick and had to go home.

Some wag said she must be sick to have bought the ugly jug and she was then stopped from leaving by a very dapper chap wearing a suit and with a silk scarf round his neck — obviously a dealer looking for bargains. He tried to grasp the jug and offered Penny 150FF for it.

She kept hold of it quite firmly and declined his offer equally firmly.

"Told you I'd done the right thing," she said, turning to the gathering, who gawped. "I'll get double that in Paris next week."

And with that, she swept off.

We left Villecroze and the *Brocante* behind us and took the excellent lunch with us to Chris and Wendy's house, Bastide St Jacques, just on the edge of Seyne town.

A *bastide*, I was to discover, is one down from a *château*, just above a *manoir*, and I'd seen it briefly from the outside when picking something up from Chris after my first experience of market days in Seyne. It is truly magnificent, the facade breathtakingly noble and when you step inside your breath is seriously taken.

Chris and Wendy have spent four years on a steady restoration project which is still on-going, and he took much delight in showing Mother and me around. The engineer in him was truly on display as he pointed out how each tile, each piece of wood, each door had been carefully replaced or re-cycled. One door, he explained, he'd found on a rubbish dump. A man after my own heart. A fellow *poubelle*-peeper.

The hallway floor is a tiled mosaic of the Mediterranean Sea and its surrounding countries at the time of the Crusades and Chris explained that this part of the *bastide*, the oldest, was some kind of Lodge or meeting place. Out in the garden is a walled walkway, the walls of which are engraved from top to bottom with some kind of Latin encyclopedia. It's a truly magnificent place and one to which I must turn the Marsh attention when I return to Seyne, which I surely will.

All my life people have questioned my sanity. I wish to spend a lot of what remains in Seyne.

*

I took Mother to Pruniers and Tourtour just for old times' sake and to kill the time between *Brocante* and the next market day, I even took her for a short sail.

She wanted to go out on Rip-Rap and I'd said I would pick the day and the time. It was perfect, we couldn't have had a better wind, just enough to push Rip-Rap along, and we made it into my lagoon where the tent was rigged and a picnic devoured. I think Mother was suitably impressed and we only had one gusty moment on the way back.

Fortunately she was on the toilet at the time and didn't notice.

There are surprisingly few birds on and around the lake, of the feathered variety that is, apart from a couple who strutted up and down the pontoon and who sometimes came aboard to peck at the remains of my *baguette*.

A few seagulls would be seen floating around, but one thing I was thankful for was not having to clean up the decks every time I came to the boat. That's one disadvantage of sea yottin', seagull shit on your decks and boom cover.

I've never been much of a naturalist and therefore not much good at spotting types of birds, but I'm better than Tom. Tom is the chap I first did off-shore yottin' of any length with, in his Splinter 21, Glasson Dock to the Isle of Man or Holyhead, that sort of thing. I used to ask him what kind of bird I'd spotted and without looking up he'd say,

"Shag."

Occasionally, the reply would vary, like the time I asked him what kind of bird was it I'd just seen, the one with the white body and black head.

"A white bodied shag, wi' a black 'ead." came the reply.

It always amused me, so much so that at one time I'd nearly purchased a Seabird, a class of yacht much favoured in the Thirties and still sailed at such places as Abersoch. They all have romantic names like 'Kittywake', 'Cormorant' or 'Puffin'.

I was going to call mine 'Shag'.

I can safely say however, with all confidence, that I never

spotted a shag on Le Lac de Sainte Serre, black headed or otherwise, until that day Mother came out for a sail with me.

On the way back we had to hug the shore in order to take advantage of what little wind there was and I was fascinated by two peculiarly shaped sticks on the shoreline. The water level was right down by late August, ten or so metres less than in June, and all manner of things started appearing, mainly rocks where I hadn't realised there were any rocks, but these sticks were a mystery. I pointed them out to Mother and asked what she thought they might be.

"Shags," she said.

Tom, I had always felt was a bit dippy, Mother definitely is. I started to laugh and then suddenly the sticks took flight. They flapped low over the water and disappeared across the lake. Two black shags.

For the first two days of Mother's holiday I'd checked her into the only place with a room available, a hotel high on a hill over-looking the lake on the southern shore. She took some snaps as Rip-Rap glided past and muttered something about how beautiful the place was. I think she'd wanted to stay there, but it's very isolated so I'd moved her into the *auberge*, right in the middle of Brouville village, where she could wander around on her own and give me a little space.

Market day dawned and the Volvo headed once more towards Seyne. Mother was plonked next to Danny, a much travelled gent who was much taken with her.

It's strange how one always thinks other people's mothers are much nicer than one's own and Danny proved to be no exception. For two hours they were huddled in deep conversation and on the market day after Mother's departure for England, he spent a great deal of time regaling the assembled company with Mother's tales, many of which I'd never heard.

Quite a character is Danny, and on this day we had a completely different gathering of folk, most of the usual gang having taken themselves off to Italy to cause mayhem and mirth over the border for a few days. It was a small but elite group who, for a change, invaded Le Grand for a terrace lunch and we feasted the afternoon away on the most magnificent seafood salad. I was to discover that Danny not only has a large house in Seyne, where this group were all staying, he also has places in London and Marrakesh.

The afternoon was rounded off by Danny picking up the meal tab and me picking up a female German hitch-hiker and taking her out for a sail on Rip-Rap, then later being treated to a decent bottle of wine for my trouble.

What a life, eh?

Chapter 13

FULL CIRCLE

*In which I tell of taking a delightful gaggle of
girls out for a day's yottin' and get a visit from
the Gendarmes. I also summarise the tale
and return home.*

"Do you know I've had eleven men in eleven months!"
Martine was opening her heart to me.

I'm as good a sounding board as you'll find for that sort of
thing, having been ditched a few times myself and after Martine's
chap had done the dirty a couple of months before, she'd actively
gone about finding a replacement for the hapless Yves. That
involved writing off to a couple of dozen hopefuls from some eco
dating agency she belonged to. I knew this because she'd asked
me to post the bulky parcel off and when I'd casually enquired as
to its contents she'd told me, quite honestly and openly. Seems
she'd being doing this for some years, ever since her divorce in
fact, and all the way through her relationship with Yves who she'd
also met in this manner. Poor lad, he was better off without her.

"As lovers?"

My curiosity was up.

"No!" she giggled. "Just dates. I like to find out a bit about the
man before that."

"Well you'd better make it twelve in that case."

"Why twelve?"

"Me. You've got to know a little bit about me and we've never
been in the sack together, yet."

She giggled again and said:

"But you are not suitable, not for me."

"I know Martine, and I'm thankful for small mercies."

Being the twelfth in eleven months would be a trifle worrying if
she had ended up in the sack with them, eco dates or not.

"I'm not for you because I smoke and drink and eat red meat
and snore and fart and besides I'm fixed up already, thanks to

191

Mother."

She looked at me in thoughtful silence for a few moments and then said:

"No. But you've got nice legs."

She glanced down at the knobbly brown knees sticking out of my yottin' shorts and giggled again.

"That's a sweeping statement," I said. "You've only seen two of them."

It'd been a good summer all in all, blissfully free of being sweatily pressed against female flesh. Seen plenty, touched none, but now I was eager to return to England and gaze fondly into those beautiful greeny-blue eyes I'd been missing so badly.

My telephone chats with Beth had become less frequent after the first flush of loneliness had prompted a call a day. Besides, it was bloody expensive, fifty units whizzing by in a matter of minutes, even at cheap rate time. I think we'd managed to keep the candle burning, it was hard to tell with Beth, she can be such a taciturn sort at times. I wouldn't blame her for latching on to another chap, it wouldn't be difficult, but I was hoping that she'd remained true and we could take up where we'd left off. No matter what, we'd perhaps remain good pals. I'd managed to do just that with a couple of Beth's predecessors and saw no reason why it shouldn't be so with her. I'd even fixed one of them up with one of my mates. How pally can you get?

Some of the female flesh I had much enjoyed seeing, at rather closer quarters than most, was that possessed by the five girls who came aboard Rip-Rap for a memorable afternoon's eighteenth birthday celebration.

No sooner had we left the pontoon than they took it in turns to dive into the cabin and re-appear one by one clad in nothing more than skimpy bikini bottoms. I turned the boat rather closer than usual to Brouville beach, as two of the nearly naked lovelies made their way up to the foredeck and draped themselves over it. This manoeuvre enabled the entire population of the beach and perhaps Brouville to see and appreciate what a lucky man I was and had the added advantage of showing the bovine Breton just what an unlucky stupid, thick and useless piece of cow-shit he was. Free pedalo, indeed, he was up against serious opposition here and when I saw his eyes popping out as Rip-Rap slid gracefully by his pitch, I thought he was going to have a fit. I raised my beer can and waved to him, before hoisting the spinnaker and making rapid progress towards my secluded little lagoon.

I cannot remember a moment I've savoured quite as much as that one.

The girls all turned out to be absolutely delightful, two of them particularly.

Nicole, whose birthday treat this was and Anne-Marie who had done some dinghy sailing with her dad, couldn't keep their hands off pulling bits of string and tweaking Rip-Rap into faster ways. The middle stump of the Marsh wicket was doing a fair bit of tweaking too, and it was all I could do to keep my hands on the tiller.

We made the lagoon in short order and the hook was dropped. The girls partied the afternoon away, alternating between swimming and sunbathing, drinking and feasting on the superb picnic I'd had François prepare and pack in the cool-box. He was mightily impressed with my pulling power and I think a tad on the jealous side. Katrine had stayed away, but once or twice a week he'd go to see his family and he was gradually coming to terms with being single again, despite the fact that his recently widowed mother turned up to house-keep for him.

I could tell he was missing Milko too, they'd been a solid double act for some years and were close friends, but all good things must come to an end, like that afternoon.

Finally tiring of the jet-set life I'd introduced them to, the girls pulled on T-shirts, pulled up the anchor and Rip-Rap pulled out of the lagoon and back across the lake towards Brouville.

As we circled round the pontoon I noticed a group of uniformed men standing on it and guessed that this must be reinforcements from the Pumped-up Soppy Ones HQ. No big fire was in evidence however, the sky and water being thankfully free of Les

Kamikazes, and as we moved closer I saw that these were definitely not Soppy Ones — they had guns.

"*Gendarmes,*" said Nikki. "What do they want?"

The four boys in blue were glaring steadfastly at me, as Rip-Rap nosed in, and one of the girls got onto the pontoon with my mooring line.

"Who, not what, Nikki. They want me."

I had no doubt whatsoever that le crunch had come. I'd been worded up good and proper, and I also had little doubt by whom.

All manner of thoughts tumbled through my mind. I had never breathed a word of my chartering at the campsite, not to Stef or Stephanie or anyone else. I hadn't even said anything to François for that matter. He genuinely thought I was taking friends for a jolly and then repairing with them to the Café. I'd even introduced them as friends, so Martine and I were the only ones who knew and the people who'd come out with me. Had one of them said something? Or had the bovine Breton done some detective work? His byre was but 20 metres from Martine's gaff at the reception and next door to Le Cab. He could have overheard some tit-bit, put two and two together and waited for his moment to pounce.

"Good gentlenoon, aftermen. Can I gee of service?" I said, stepping off the bows and onto the pontoon, desperately trying to disguise my fear.

My moist hands trembled and inwardly, my stomach churned. A rapidly drying mouth made comprehensible speech just a tad on the hard side.

"*Monsieur* Marsh?" enquired the uniform with the most glittery things on, smiling politely.

"*Oui,*" I smiled politely back.

"*Parlez-vous Francais?*"

"*Non.*"

"I will translate," said Nikki, who had followed me to the bows and now jumped down onto the pontoon.

There followed an earnest discussion between Nicole and the

uniform. Not once was I brought into the conversation, although I was mentioned quite a few times.

The gist of it was that the *Gendarme* was asking if the girls had paid me to be taken out on the boat and Nikki and all the other girls, who'd gathered round, vehemently denied that they had, not a single *franc*, that I had invited them as a birthday treat, had provided them with all the drink and food and I had never even mentioned money. Finally she turned to me and said:

"The officer wants to know if you have ever charged people to be taken out on Rip-Rap."

"Absolutely not. Never." My usual strength of character was returning, despite the imminent threat of arrest and imprisonment. "Will you please tell the officer that I am very aware that to do so would be against the law. Please also tell him that I had discussions with the *Maire de* Brouville with a view to chartering but realised I would not be allowed to do so without registering my activities and as that was very complex and expensive I decided not to do it and if he would like confirmation of that fact, please ask the *Maire*."

Nikki started to tell him what I'd said but he held his hand up and interrupted her. The *Gendarme* turned to me, bowed his head courteously with a smile and then said, in perfect English:

"It seems you have made some people very jealous, *Monsieur* Marsh, and I am not surprised with such a beautiful boat and equally beautiful sailing companions. I am sorry to have troubled you. Good day."

And with that he turned and ushered the troops away.

I climbed back aboard Rip-Rap and sat down in the cockpit.

All the girls joined me and seemed very subdued. The attentions of the boys in blue can be a nerve-racking experience and every nerve I had was on the rack. The vision of Rip-Rap being chained to the pontoon and weeks, months or years of learning all the French laws in some stinking, rat-infested jail was too much to bear.

"Fetch us some beers up, Anne-Marie. The party's not over yet."

I didn't know about them, but I was in need of some serious shoring-up.

The girls came back to life, but the party was over and they wanted to get back to Le Camping and shower and change. They thanked me profusely, each kissing me in turn, Nikki first and last, and they left me sitting on my own in the cockpit, beer in hand as the sun went down.

It was time to call a halt to the chartering side of things — that had been a very close call indeed. I was just thankful that the shit-thick bovine Breton had chosen that particular day to grass me up to *les flics*.

Apart from Mother, Martine, Dave, Milko and one or two others, I had charged a modest amount each time, just enough to cover a meal or two, with *un demi de rouge* of course.

I suppose that after that incident the boys in blue would probably have left me alone had anybody else tried to drop me in the proverbial. They had questioned me and were satisfied that I was well above the law. Amazingly they hadn't even asked to see any paperwork, boat registration, my ICC, nothing. To them I was just an eccentric rich Englishman spending the summer indulging himself in a fanciful whim. That was the impression I suppose I'd given, although far from the truth.

Fact of the matter was that by late August I was skint, my meagre savings having been eaten into and exhausted. I'd even had to arrange a bank loan to tide me over.

I'd worked out before I left for France that I could live on £10 a day, the worst case scenario without earning from charters, but the reality was it cost £20 or more, with the caravan rent and pontoon charges taken into account. Extra were things like Luke's holiday which turned out to be an expensive week, but I didn't begrudge a penny of that. Also not included were the ferry fares and petrol, all of which were paid for by credit card and would have to be faced upon my return.

So, all-in-all a bloody expensive, fanciful whim.

"There you go, Bruno. I think that's everything."

I handed him the boat keys and ordered more coffee. We were sitting outside the Café du Soleil and Bruno had offered to pull

Rip-Rap out of the water with his Range Rover. We'd waited three days for the wind to drop sufficiently to make this operation as safe as possible — Bruno knows just how much I think of Rip-Rap and how much care I take of her. It was not to be and I was anxious to get home. However, I had all confidence in Bruno and his cohorts at *le Club Nautique* and I'd arranged winter storage there some weeks before. She would be locked onto the locked trailer and locked up in *le Club* compound. Total cost £50, including being pulled out and launched again next spring. Incredibly cheap, when compared to boat storage prices in the UK, and I didn't have to face the long journey home and the increased fuel and ferry costs.

I still hadn't decided what to do about the next season and planned to think about it over the winter. Many plans were afoot, one of them being the delivery of Gazzer's Picnic to the Med, so there was the possibility that I could take Rip-Rap there. After all, she's only 80 miles away from the Med, so my ultimate dream may come true.

After the ceremonial handing over of the keys, an up-market bottle of *pastis*, a Rip-Rap polo shirt and the 500FF for the boat storage, we shook hands and I departed, after saying my good-byes to François and Milko, who had returned to work at the Café and see out the end-of-season period.

Mid September, and Brouville was once more grockle-free and practically deserted. I then returned to the campsite to settle up with Martine.

Some days before she had negotiated with the *Mairie* and I was to be charged for only the three months I had stayed there instead of the four originally planned and booked for me by François. That was a huge relief. I handed her the 4500FF, then she hit me with a bombshell.

"You are to pay the local taxes, they say, as you have been resident here."

"God Almighty, old girl. I've hardly any French money left."

Early that morning I'd packed my belongings into the Volvo, driven to Seyne and drawn 5000FF out of the hole-in-the-wall to cover the campsite and boat storage charges. Now, all I had left was a 100 *franc* note and some loose change to cover the odd cup of coffee and sandwich on the journey. Autoroute tolls, I had discovered, could be paid by credit card.

"You want me to pay the taxes for you?"

"Damned generous of you, Martine. How much is it?"

"Twenty eight *francs.*"

I burst out laughing.

"Twenty eight *francs*! No, I think I can stretch to that."

I handed her the money out of my loose change and thought of the irony of me becoming a French taxpayer. £2.80 wasn't really a huge penalty to pay for my summer sojourn.

It was an emotional parting. Martine and I had shared much that summer and I was determined that we should remain good friends. After all, her house could come in useful as accommodation for a WANCAs yottin' trip to Le Lac, which I had planned for the following spring.

It took seventeen and a half hours to drive home, the return journey that had taken four days the other way. A non-stop, single-handed stint, non-stop that is, apart from petrol and pee stops and the hour's wait for the ferry. It was 3.30 the next morning when I let myself into the cottage and poured myself a large duty-free Scotch. I felt I had deserved it and I was still on a buzz after the thousand-mile trip. I think it was about a thousand: I couldn't tell you for sure as the Volvo's mileometer had ceased to work after 187.1 miles of the trip and only started turning again as I turned off the M6 and headed for Macclesfield and home.

That lunchtime I popped into my usual local in order to catch up with all the gossip, but nothing much had happened and nothing much had changed.

My solicitor was in attendance and informed me that my dispute with Visa and Lo-Cost Rent-a-Car, although having been settled in principle before my departure, had not, in fact, been settled in reality. We discussed a course of action and he promised to put it in hand on his return to the office the following Monday.

In two weeks' time it would be exactly a year since this little adventure had begun. Full circle, I suppose. I was nearly 54 and still had all the sense of an 18 year old.

I had learned a lot though, and I still had Beth. That evening she came round to my cottage and we went out for a curry, something else I hadn't had the pleasure of for three months. I gazed into those greeny-blue eyes, the colour so reminiscent of the waters I'd spent a large part of my summer on, and promised myself that I'd never go away again.

Yet!

FIN

GLOSSARY OF YOTTSPEAK

WANCAs and their craft
Dave (Big and/or Daft) & Pauline – *Trenarth* (Nicholson 31)
Duncan (Dunc) & Louise (Padded Shoulders) – *Rufus* (Hunter
Duette)
Gary (Gaz or Gazzer) – *Picnic* (Nicholson 31), previously *Hunca
Munca* (Evolution 26)
Neil & Randi – *Aquarius* (Elizabethan 23)
Peter & Luke – *Rip-Rap* (Friendship 22)
Tim – *Black Dog* (modified Poacher 21)
Tony & Tina – *Fenella* (Folkboat)
Various others, full or part-time WANCA crew members

BOAT TYPES
SLOOP – single masted monohull
KETCH – two-masted monohull, front mast taller than mizzen mast
SCHOONER – two-masted monohull, front mast usually shorter
than mizzen mast
DINGHY – tender to big boat, or small sailing craft usually used for
racing
DORY – twin-skinned dinghy, very stable and rectangular in shape
RIB – Rigid Inflatable Boat, solid floor with inflatable sausage sides
SMACK – fishing boat

BOAT BITS
AFT – rear
ANCHOR – obvious really, sometimes referred to as 'hook'
AWNING – see 'boom tent'
BABYSTAY – part of rigging, from 2/3 up front of mast to approx
middle of foredeck
BACKSTAY – part of rigging, from top of mast to transom
BAGGYWRINKLES – devices around the shrouds at their junction
with the spreaders, traditionally rope, which protect head
sails from chaffing
BERTH – bunk (on boat), mooring place (in harbour)
BILGE KEELS – two things sticking out of the bottom, essential for
balance of the boat

GLOSSARY OF YOTTSPEAK

BLOCK – pulley wheel

BOAT-HOOK – pole with hook on one end, mostly used for picking up mooring

BOOM – spar at 90 degrees to mast, holding foot of mainsail

BOOM TENT – awning which is draped over boom and provides shelter from sun and rain

BOW – sharp end of craft, sometimes referred to as 'bows'

CABIN – inside of boat, sometimes called 'saloon'

CAST OFF – drop mooring lines prior to leaving berth or mooring

CENTREBOARD – single drop keel

CLEAT – device which secures ropes and sheets

COACHROOF – top of cabin, raised above deck level

COCKPIT – well in which one sits, usually at rear of boat

COMPANIONWAY – steps descending from cockpit to cabin

COMPASS – magnetic thing showing directions

CROSS-TREES – see 'spreaders'

DRAUGHT – distance between waterline and bottom of keel

DONKEY – engine, or motor

DUCKBOARDS – raised, slatted wooden floor covering, allowing water to drain beneath

ECHO-SOUNDER – instrument used to measure depth of water beneath boat

FENDER – sausage shaped rubber do-dah dangled over the side to prevent damage caused by bumping into things

FIN KEEL – single thing sticking out of the bottom, essential for balance of the boat

FORE – front

FOREDECK – roof of forepeak, front deck

FOREPEAK – front cabin

FORESTAY – part of rigging, from top of mast to bow

GALLEY – kitchen area in cabin

GPS – Global Positioning System, satellite controlled instrument which gives position

GUARDRAIL – safety wire running along sides of deck from pulpit to pushpit at height of approx 2 feet

GUNWALE – top of the sides of boat

GUY – rope which is attached to spinnaker and onto which the pole is clipped

HALYARD – rope for hauling up sails, through pulley usually located at top of mast

HATCH – sliding or folding cover of aperture

HEADS – toilet facilities

HEADSAIL – (see 'Sails' below)

HELM – see 'tiller'

HOOK – anchor

JAMMER – type of cleat, usually cam-cleat, secures sheets etc

JIB – another word for 'headsail'

KEEL – (see 'bilge', 'fin', 'skeg')

KICKER – (or vang) tensioning device beneath boom at angle approx 45 degrees to foot of mast

KNOT – thing you tie, or one nautical mile per hour

LAZY-JACKS – rope device which facilitates the mainsail to furl itself onto boom when lowered

LOCKER – compartment for stowing stuff

LOG – instrument which reads speed and distance travelled, usually driven by paddle under boat

MAINSHEET – rope which controls movement of the boom and mainsail

MAST – thing that sticks up (sometimes referred to as 'the stick')

MASTHEAD – top of mast

MIZZEN MAST – rear mast on ketch or schooner

PAINTER – rope on front of boat, used for tying boat to something

PULPIT – solid guardrail around bow

PUSHPIT – solid guardrail around transom

RIGGING – wires which support mast

ROLLER-REEFING – furling device, rotating sail-track on forestay wrapping headsail around

RUDDER – plank sticking down rear of boat which when moved steers the vessel

SAIL – see 'Sails' below

SAIL WARDROBE – complement of sails carried aboard

SEXTANT – instrument used when determining position using astro-navigation

SHEET – rope attached to sail which controls tension and curve of sail (sometimes called 'string')

SHOCK CORD – rubberised stretchy cord

SHROUD – part of rigging, from top of mast to either side of deck

SKEG – stubby keel

SOLE BOARD – cabin floor

SPINNAKER POLE – pole rigged on front of mast which acts as 'boom' for the spinnaker (see 'Sails')

SPREADERS – (or cross-trees) struts sticking out of side of mast which hold and locate shrouds

STANCHION – upright metal pole, usually those which hold guardrail

STERN – see 'transom'

STICK – mast (sometimes 'tiller')

STRING – see 'sheet'

THWART – seat in dinghy

TILLER – (or helm) stick attached to rudder to facilitate steering

TOE-RAIL – raised strip running along top side of deck from fore to aft

TOPPING LIFT – rope from top of mast to outer end of boom

TRANSOM – (or 'stern') rear end of boat

TRAVELLER – track running across cockpit which controls movement of mainsheet

UPHAUL/DOWNHAUL – two ropes above and below spinnaker pole which set the pole in position

VHF – ship-to-shore radio (Very High Frequency)

WASHBOARDS – tapered boards slotted into tracks on either side of entrance from cockpit to cabin

WARPS – ropes used as mooring lines

WINCH – windlass, mostly used for tensioning sheets

SAILS

GENNAKER– (or 'cruising chute') cross between Genoa and Spinnaker

GENOA – (or 'jennie') large headsail

HEADSAIL – any sail in front of mast, held in track on forestay

MAINSAIL – behind mast, held in tracks on mast and boom

MIZZEN – rear sail on ketch or schooner

SLOTSAIL – in front of mast, behind headsail, held in track on babystay

SPINNAKER – ('spinnie' or 'kite') usually very colourful sail which billows out the front

STORM JIB – small headsail used in very strong winds

OTHER YOTTIE EXPRESSIONS

ALMANAC – an annual publication containing comprehensive navigational and other nautical details

ANTI-FOULING – special paint on hull below waterline.

BEAM ENDS, ON HER – boat heeled over through 90 degrees

BEAT – sailing upwind

BOWLINE - (pronounced 'bo-lyn') a type of knot

BUOY – thing that floats and denotes or marks something

CHANDLER – person who purveys yottie bits and bobs

CHANDLERY – shop in which chandler conducts his trade

DELIVERY – (or repositioning) taking boat from one place to another

EAR, RIGHT ON HER – see 'beam ends'

FAIRWAY BUOY – mark which denotes entrance to deep water channel in estuary

FLEET – group of boats in same racing class

GROCKLES – tourists, usually landlubbers

GYBE – altering direction downwind

HANDICAP – rating given to racing craft, calculated by measuring dimensions of hull, sails etc

HELM, OR HELMSMAN – crew member who steers boat

HONK – wind, blowing hard or chucking up (spewing)

HOOLIE - (abbr. for 'hooligan') very strong wind, usually Storm Force

MARK – buoy denoting rounding point on racing course

M.O.B. – Man Over Board

MOORING – large plastic ball attached to seabed by chain and anchors to which you tie your boat

NAVIGATOR – crew member who plots course

OFF WATCH – period of time spent below deck whilst yottin'

OGGIE – (slang: ocean) the water on which we yott

OILIES – (abbr. for 'oilskins') waterproof clothing

ON WATCH – period of time spent on deck whilst yottin'

PICK-UP – small plastic ball with hand grip, attached to mooring

PILOT BOOK – reference book giving navigational information of specific sailing areas

PONTOON – floating walkway to which you tie boats

PORT – left

PROTEST – action taken when one or more boats have been considered to infringe racing rules

RAIL, ON THE – dangling ones legs over the side to aid balance of
   boat
REACH – sailing across the wind
RED DUSTER – flag, Red Ensign
REEF – to shorten sails, a type of knot or rocky outcrop
ROUND THE CANS – shortish race which takes place on a course
   marked by buoys
RUN – sailing downwind
SSR – Small Ships Register
STARBOARD – right
STEP – erect the mast, rig it
TACK – altering direction to windward
TACTICIAN – crew member who decides race tactics
TRANSIT – two objects, usually poles on shore which, when lined
   up, denote start and/or finish line of race
TRAVEL HOIST – large crane with slings, used for launching and
   retrieval of boats
UNSTEP – take mast down, de-rig
WATCH ABOVE – crew members 'on watch'
WATCH BELOW – crew members 'off watch'
WAYPOINT – position of destination or change of direction in a
   course